Multicultural
Plays
for Children

VOLUME II: GRADES 4–6

Smith and Kraus *Books For Actors*
YOUNG ACTORS SERIES

Great Scenes and Monologues for Children
Great Scenes for Young Actors from the Stage
Great Monologues for Young Actors
Multicultural Monologues for Young Actors
Multicultural Scenes for Young Actors
Monologues from Classic Plays 468 BC to 1960 AD
Scenes from Classic Plays 468 BC to 1970 AD
New Plays from A.C.T.'s Young Conservatory Vol. I
New Plays from A.C.I.'s Young Conservatory Vol. II
Plays of America from American Folklore for Young Actors 7-12
Seattle Children's Theatre: Six Plays for Young Actors
Short Plays for Young Actors
Villeggiatura: A Trilogy by Carlo Goldoni, *condensed for Young Actors*
Loving to Audition: The Audition Workbook for Young Actors
Movement Stories for Children
An Index of Plays for Young Actors
Discovering Shakespeare: A Midsummer Night's Dream,
    A Workbook for Students
Discovering Shakespeare: Romeo and Juliet, *A Workbook*
    for Students
Discovering Shakespeare: The Taming of the Shrew,
    A Workbook for Students

CAREER DEVELOPMENT SERIES

The Job Book: 100 Acting Jobs for Actors
The Job Book II: 100 Day Jobs for Actors
The Smith and Kraus Monologue Index
The Great Acting Teachers and Their Methods
The Actor's Guide to Qualified Acting Coaches: New York
The Actor's Guide to Qualified Acting Coaches: Los Angeles
The Camera Smart Actor
The Sanford Meisner Approach
Cold Readings: Some Do's and Don'ts for Actors at Auditions

If you require pre-publication information about upcoming Smith and Kraus books, you may receive our semi-annual catalogue, free of charge, by sending your name and address to *Smith and Kraus Catalogue, P.O. Box 127, One Main Street, Lyme, NH 03768. Or call us at (800) 895-4331, fax (603) 795-4427.*

Multicultural Plays for Children

for Children

VOLUME II: GRADES 4–6

by Pamela Gerke

Young Actors Series

SK

A Smith and Kraus Book

A Smith and Kraus Book
Published by Smith and Kraus, Inc.
One Main Street, PO Box 127, Lyme, NH 03768

Copyright ©1996 by Pamela Gerke All rights reserved
Manufactured in the United States of America
Cover and Text Design by Julia Hill
Cover Art by Irene Kelly
First Edition: March 1996
10 9 8 7 6 5 4 3 2 1

Library of Congress Cataloging-In-Publication Data
Gerke, Pamela.
Multicultural plays for young actors / by Pamela Gerke.
p. cm. -- (Young actors series)
Includes bibliographical references.
Contents: v. 2. Grade levels 4-6.
Summary: Ten plays based on multicultural folktales from such
countries as Ghana, China, and Italy.
ISBN 1-57525-006-3 (v.2)
1. Pluralism (Social sciences--Juvenile drama.) 2. Ethnic groups--Juvenile drama.
3. Children's plays, American. 4. Drama in education.
[1. Folklore-Drama. 2. Plays.] I. Title. II. Series.
PS3557.E674M85   1996
812'.54--dc20   96-164
CIP
AC

Acknowledgements

Thanks to all the people who helped me with foreign language translations and pronunciations and cultural information: Stesha Brandon, Inga Furlong, Maria Gillman, Vi Hilbert, Stacia Keogh, Eileen Kilgren, Nancy Mar, David Miles, Vladimir Vladimirov, Rae Wu and Louise Zamporutti.

Thanks for computer support to: Phyllis Roberts, Allan Tamm and Richard Weeks.

Thanks to all the kids who were involved in the original productions of these scripts.

Dedicated to Mud, Mary L. Gerke, with love.

Contents

WORKING WITH CHILDREN
IN PLAY PRODUCTION *(Cont.)*

PREFACE by Vi Hilbert

THE SCRIPTS

BIBLIOGRAPHY

Introduction

This book is designed for use by classroom teachers and other adults who work with children and want to do plays with them. Each script comes with detailed suggestions for creating all the elements of production: sets, props, costumes, lights, and sound, as well as staging directions, vocabulary lists of foreign language words used in the scripts, and general information about how to alter and adapt each script for various circumstances (cast size, rehearsal time, number of girls or boys in the cast, and so forth). Included in the introductions to the plays are discussions on the subject of the significance of play production as a child development activity, including psychological, emotional, kinesthetic, social, and educational aspects. Also included in this book are general instructions and suggestions for working with children in play productions.

I began to write and direct children's plays several years ago when I was directing an after-school program at an elementary school. At the time it seemed to be one of the most fun things we could do—and it was! I then created a children's play production company, Kids Action Theater, where I've written, directed, and produced all of the plays in this book. Working with children in play production continues to be a source of artistic inspiration, pleasure, and income for me and the old adage still rings true: By working with children, I learn about myself.

I believe that as citizens of the twenty-first century it is imperative that we integrate the arts into our educational systems. Our Western culture and education have been biased toward so-called "left brain" thinking for far too long. If we are to truly fulfill our human potential, stop the destruction of our environment, and create a sustainable, peaceful community, we must develop whole-brain thinking skills. To do this, the arts and other creative, nonlinear, nondualistic ways of thinking and being must be given at least as much attention in our schools as the modes of thinking that are traditionally emphasized.

The Significance of
Play Production
in Child Development

HUMAN DEVELOPMENT AND THE MEANING OF FUN

I believe our human system is designed so as to make us want to do that which is good for our own development. This is particularly noticeable in children. We can learn about what is good nourishment for children's development by observing what it is that they *want* to do, what is fun for them. They want to swing on swings and spin on merry-go-rounds because such repetitive movements aid in neurological patterning and the development of the vestibular system and equilibrium. Children want to climb on jungle gyms because it's good for their gross motor and brain development to do so. They want to be watched and praised because it helps them develop a positive self-image.

Children, allowed to play freely, will most often choose to dramatize their fantasies—to playact. Children playact because it's fun, and I say it's fun because it's psychologically, emotionally, and kinesthetically good for them. Playacting allows children to experience being in complete control of their world, where they can successfully solve problems and creatively express their feelings and desires.

PSYCHOLOGICAL ASPECTS

Working with children in play production is good for their development. It allows them to be physically active and learn kinesthetically, i.e., through their bodies. Plays create safe situations where children can act out adventure, danger, combat, and even death. The experience of fantasy, imagery, symbolism, and movement speaks to the psyche, invoking primal instincts, playing out archetypal roles, and satisfying unconscious needs to resolve problems. Plays can creatively address what one of my teachers, Molly Scudder, calls the "tender topics": sex, violence and death, subjects which we in our Western society seem to avoid with children but which they are often greatly concerned with coming to terms with. Play productions give children the opportunity to take risks, act in ways that would otherwise not be "allowed" in real life, and express hidden feelings.

ATTENTION, SELF-ESTEEM & PERSONAL EMPOWERMENT

Producing plays with children helps them learn to focus their attention, one of the most important tasks of child development. As is true for adults, it's a lot easier to pay attention when what you are doing is enjoyable, and playacting is one of the most fun activities of all for children.

Play production is also a natural device for positive "mirroring," reflecting back to children support from which they can build a good self-image. As they take their bows, being watched and literally applauded for their good efforts, children beam with pleasure and receive a big, healthy boost to their self-esteem.

Play productions help develop what Mary Budd Rowe calls "fate control," that is, the belief that individuals have control over the events in their lives. In the realm of the arts there is really no "right and wrong" as established by an external authority (critics included!). Drama and other arts activities can help children realize their own, internal powers of imagination and personal truth and a sense of control over their lives if the adults working with them allow them to freely express their ideas and share ownership of the creation of the play production.

ARTS EDUCATION

All arts activities have the power to connect to the inner depths of the psyche through imagination, symbolism, and humor. The arts need to be recognized as equal to all other subjects in our educational system. Arts activities support learning styles and brain functions which are otherwise mostly neglected in our schools but that are vital to the development of creative thinking, a balanced personality, and a healthy psyche. The arts can be integrated with other subjects to promote whole-brain thinking. Literature, reading, social studies, history, foreign language, music, movement and art are some of the subjects covered by producing the plays in this book.

Collaborative arts activities, such as plays, help children to develop good social skills. Artistic collaboration calls for group decision making and cooperation in order to be successful. In addition, there's a certain sense of comradery that naturally develops among a cast that warms and strengthens their social interactions.

FOLK TALES & MULTICULTURAL EDUCATION

All the plays in this books are adaptations of folktales from various countries or cultures from around the world. These are stories that have been handed down through the ages, continually altered and adapted by succeeding generations while retaining core truths about human nature and existence. Folktales, fairytales, and myths are stories that have lasted because they speak of profound truths, teach us about life and ethics, and are vastly entertaining. With the proliferation of commercial entertainment in our modern, Western culture, we are losing an important psychological and social tool in the form of folktales and mythology.

Producing plays of folktales is a good way to study other groups of people, their culture, language, literature, traditions and wisdom. Teaching children these ancient stories helps in their moral and spiritual development, spreads cultural literacy, cross-cultural awareness and understanding, and promotes a high level of artistic quality.

Working with Children in Play Productions

DIRECTOR'S ATTITUDE

Besides all the serious and profound reasons for doing plays with kids, the most important thing is: It's just plain fun! And if the adults maintain a playful attitude, they will enjoy it as much as the kids.

I'll never forget when my attitude was first altered regarding this. I was directing a play with four- to six- year-olds and as we approached performance day, I became increasingly frustrated and angry with the cast for not living up to my demands for perfection. The day came when I lost my temper and threatened to cancel the performance. All of a sudden, in the middle of my tirade, little Oscar projectile vomited. Bright orange and pink vomit went spewing out of his mouth and all over the stage and in that moment I realized that nothing really mattered (except Oscar's well-being). Since then, whenever I'm directing a children's play and begin to feel angry, wanting the production to meet my (adult) standards of perfection, I remember Oscar and the bright orange and pink projectile vomit and my sense of perspective and priority is righted.

Directing plays with children can be a very satisfying and enjoyable experience. But if you, the director, are not clear about what your goals are and what you expect from your cast members, the play experience can become frustrating and nerve-wracking. Ideally, the purpose of doing plays with children should be to provide an enriching, educational, and fun experience and one that promotes self-esteem. You, too, will also learn from and enjoy this experience if you focus on these goals.

It's understandable if you, as director, become anxious and demanding in rehearsals due to your desire to have the production meet your standards of excellence and your sense of responsibility for it's outcome. The best thing you can do is to maintain a positive, relaxed attitude at all times and always be fully supportive of every member of your cast and crew. Keep the production in perspective:

Remember, it's not Broadway—it's a bunch of kids doing their best and hopefully having fun in the process.

At the same time, expect nothing but the best from your actors. Demand that they pay attention, cooperate with others and try their hardest. Maintain a rehearsal atmosphere that is disciplined and focused. Be confident in your role as leader and your cast will sense this and react accordingly, respecting your authority and the limits you set. Likewise, if you are unsure of yourself as director your cast will feel insecure and may behave badly.

One of the most difficult aspects of directing children in plays is that they sometimes have a hard time focusing on the activity, especially in the beginning. They'll be bouncing off the walls and talking more than listening, and this makes it difficult for the adults in charge. However, learning to concentrate attention is, to my mind, the most valuable reason for doing play productions with children. Their minds are not already focused on the play in the beginning of the process because focusing their attention is precisely what they have come to learn. The director should understand this and provide a supportive atmosphere for children to grow in their ability to pay attention.

Always solicit the actor's comments and suggestions for both the play and for the creation of it's production elements so that they have a sense of ownership of their play production. Encourage positive comments from the children about the work of other cast members but do not allow them to make negative comments about others because it can have a devastating effect on the other children's feelings and self-esteem.

HOW TO USE THESE SCRIPTS

These scripts are designed to be adaptable to many different situations. They can be done as an unrehearsed run-through which is not performed for an audience, wherein the teacher reads the narration and describes the action while the students act it out. These scripts can also be used as a reading activity, either unrehearsed or rehearsed for a staged reading with an audience. To do a staged reading, the actors sit in chairs facing the audience. One person reads all the stage directions as needed, and the actors read their parts and may do a minimal amount of movement, including the use of small props. Readings make interesting performances that require less preparation time than a staged production.

For fully staged productions you can alter the scripts as long as you maintain respect for the traditions from which the stories come. All the staging directions in the scripts and ideas for making sets, props, costumes, lights, sound, and music are only guidelines. Think of these ideas as simply source material from which you and your ensemble create your own, unique and creative production.

Because these scripts are all adapted from folklore of specific cultures, you can generate a lot of good ideas for your play by bringing in stories, maps, artifacts, guest speakers, current events, and other information about the culture of the play's origin and in this way use the script as the basis for an interdisciplinary social studies unit.

SCRIPT PROCEDURE

1. Make a photocopy of the entire script, including (when applicable) the foreign language vocabulary list in Appendix A.
2. After casting the play, make any changes necessary on your Master Script (see script changes below). You may want to write the names of the actors in the margin next to their characters' names. Make script changes using correction fluid or white stickers and a dark pencil or pen (black is best).
3. Make copies of your Master Script for your cast as needed. To save paper and copying cost, you can copy for each actor only the pages with their lines. If some of the actors have few or no lines to memorize, you can simply have them learn their lines by rote in rehearsal and not copy script pages for them.
4. Write the name of each cast member on their script copy and highlight their lines for them with a highlighter pen, or have them highlight their own.

SCRIPT CHANGES

1. To make a single character into a small group: Change all references to that character from singular to plural, including pronouns and (where applicable) foreign language words. The actors in the group can either say their lines in unison, or lines can be assigned to individuals (specify in the script).

2. To change a small group role into a single character: Change all references to that character from plural to singular, including pronouns and (where applicable) foreign language words. Assign all of those group lines (such as Villager #1, Villager #2, etc.) to one actor.
3. To change the gender of a character: Change all gender references to that character including pronouns and (where applicable) foreign language words.
4. To make the play shorter in length: Eliminate lines, and/or parts of scenes. The Narrator can summarize the portions that have been cut in order to retain the story line. Songs and/or dances can be eliminated.
5. To make the play longer in length: Add lines, parts of scenes, and/or scenes. New roles or scenes can be written or improvised by the actors. Songs and/or dances can be added.
6. To set the play in another country: Change all references to the location of the story, possibly including foreign language words.
7. To change the foreign language words to English, refer to the vocabulary list in Appendix A.

MEMORIZATION

I have found the best procedure for memorizing lines is to send the actors' script pages home with them, with a note to their parents/ guardians asking them to help with the memorization of lines. I ask that they spend a few minutes each day with their child, going over their lines by giving them their cues, i.e., the lines that proceed the actor's lines. I emphasize early memorization because the sooner all the lines are memorized, the better the rehearsals and productions proceed.

It's more important that the kids have a sense of the meaning of their lines than that they memorize them perfectly, word for word. Allow the actors to improvise and paraphrase. When they forget their lines, ask them what their character's intent is at that moment in the story and to describe what is really happening in the story at that point.

FOREIGN LANGUAGE

Whenever possible, ask a native speaker or other expert of the foreign language in the script you're producing to come and work with your cast, helping them learn to pronounce the words correctly, and educating your group about the country or culture being portrayed. Practice speaking the foreign language words together and wherever possible, incorporate them into the rest of your class time together. If you decide that using foreign language will create more rehearsal time than you have available, you can substitute the English translations (alter the Master Script).

CASTING

1. Read or tell the entire story of the play, using either the script or a picture book of the story. Ask the actors to be thinking about which, if any, characters they would most like to play.
2. Ask the actors to say which roles they most prefer and write their choices up on a board where everyone can see them. The actors should name all the roles they most want to play, even if others have named the same roles, or say if they are willing to play any role.
3. Review the list together and work to complete the cast list to everyone's satisfaction.

- *Whenever more than one actor wants the same role, pull names out of a hat to make the decision. I don't recommend the audition process (see below.) The exception here may be to designate that only the older children contend for lead roles that demand a lot of memorization.*
- *Roles can be changed from singular to plural or from plural to singular to accommodate your cast.*
- *The gender of roles can sometimes be changed to accommodate your cast.*

AUDITIONING

Rather than the personal choice and random selection process I recommend above, you can also audition the actors for specific roles. There is certainly something of value in auditioning, but I don't believe it's appropriate for elementary school children, especially the younger ones. At that age, children are more likely to feel "less than" if not chosen than they are to understand the auditioning process. The hurt feelings that often result from auditioning young children work against the goal of building self-esteem and make auditioning both unneccessary and inappropriate.

The personal choice and random selection process of casting accommodates everyone's choices as much as possible and treats everyone equally. The actors' choices of roles can be revealing, while playing them may prove cathartic or otherwise psychologically healing for them.

"COLOR-BLIND" & "GENDER-BLIND" CASTING

"Color-blind" casting is casting roles without regard for, or in conscious defiance of, the race or ethnic heritage of the actors as regards the roles. "Color-blind" casting can create striking, thought-provoking, and even humorous results for it illuminates assumptions about race and raises questions about how we perceive certain roles and ethnic groups.

"Gender-blind" casting does the same thing, with regard to sex role stereotypes. Often, the gender of certain characters is specific for a certain story because the story is passing on important social information about sex roles in that culture (from the past, anyway). It's important to respect all traditions and to only make changes, such as character gender, with purpose—after all, most generations change stories to adapt them to their own time and social values, and our generation can too.

For the sake of simplicity in the scripts, I've labeled each character with gender-specific pronouns and other words ("she/he" gets a bit cumbersome after awhile). These choices are often made randomly— you may change the script as needed. The introductory information for each script indicates which roles can be played as either sex, so that directors can evaluate whether or not the script will work for their particular mix of girls and boys.

Some of your actors may wish to play characters of the opposite sex. You can tell them that this is in keeping with long-standing theater tradition and respectfully accommodate their wishes whenever possible.

BLOCKING

Blocking is the planning of all basic stage placement and movements, and it's the first thing you should do before proceeding with rehearsals. This can be a tedious process, but, is well worth the patience required. Establishing the placement and movement of actors, sets, and props forms a visible framework for the play and helps to focus the work. Pay close attention to all blocking of people and things and keep an accurate record. Each movement affects other parts of the play—a misplaced prop can wreak havoc. All blocking of actors, sets, and props needs to be rehearsed as often as the lines, so it's best to get started early.

During the blocking process it's often difficult for children to pay attention and remain quiet, especially when they're not in the scene being worked on. In the beginning, they often don't understand the "big picture" and where their character fits in. Over the course of rehearsals all the pieces will come together and the play will "jell" for them. Until then, don't expect them to pay total attention when they're not in a scene and set out a quiet activity for them, such as books or drawing materials.

Stage directions are from the perspective of the actors when they're facing the audience; i.e., "right" is the actor's right. "Down" refers to the part of the stage closest to the audience and "up" is the part of the stage farthest from the audience. This is because stages used to be raked, that is, slanted down toward the audience.

AUDIENCE

DOWN LEFT	DOWN CENTER	DOWN RIGHT
LEFT	CENTER	RIGHT
UP LEFT	UP CENTER	UP RIGHT

Use many different levels for your stage, such as tabletops or other platforms, because a variety of levels makes the staging interesting. If the audience is sitting on the same level as the stage, stage your action as high up as possible, especially if the blocking calls for the actors to be sitting or lying down, because the audience in the back rows will have a hard time seeing. Use sturdy tables to your advantage as part of your acting area (and performing on tabletops will also give the kids a thrill.)

Use a lot of exciting action that's fun for the kids and it will be fun for the audience as well. Let them run, jump, skip, fly! Risk a little noise and chaos so that the actors can experience some really exciting movements. Rehearse particularly fast or chaotic action in slow motion first. Always make sure the rules are clear about how to move in the space and in relation with each other so that everyone is safe.

Repetition in blocking helps the actors remember what to do—for example: Their character always enters from a certain place and exits via a certain route. One actor can be assigned to lead group movements, which will make it easy for the others to follow. Sometimes it's useful for the actors to have an assigned order of movement, such as who goes first, second, third, and so forth, because it avoids arguments and helps the kids remember what to do.

When planning blocking, be creative with the furniture you have available. Sturdy tables with folding legs can become slides by folding up one side of the legs. Slides make for interesting movement and are, needless to say, very popular with kids. Tables, chairs, and other furniture can inspire interesting blocking as well as windows, doors, and other built-in features of your room.

Create adequate backstage areas, with enough room for the actors, sets, and props, with places where the actors can watch the play (don't place them where they can't see or hear the play). "Backstage" does not neccessarily mean that the audience can't see the actors. The actors who are not in the current scene can often be included in the scene as onlookers. This will help the kids keep their attention on the play. Make sure you plan the backstage blocking along with the on-stage blocking, so that everyone knows exactly where they're supposed to be at all times.

If you're working with a large cast, create several backstage areas with a different area assigned to each small group of characters. This will go a long way in maintaining order and quiet.

THEATER SPACE

Be creative with your performance space. The following are a few ideas:

- Place the audience around three-quarters of the stage, with you fourth portion being for backdrops, sets, or backstage.

- Create a "theater-in-the-round," where the audience sits in a circle around the stage. The feeling of intimacy can be wonderful and it eliminates the need for large sets or backdrops.
- The entire performance space, including the audience, can be decorated as the setting of the play, so that the audience is made to feel they are "in" the performance.
- Particular aspects of your building can be incorporated into the play setting, such as windows, doors, or closets.
- The performance can take place in various locations which the audience must travel to throughout the course of the play, such as the hallway, other rooms, or outside.

REHEARSALS

Rehearsals should last between thirty minutes to an hour or so. Rehearsals can be alternated with production workshops (making the sets, props, or costumes), or with music rehearsals. Always maintain a rehearsal atmosphere that is positive and fun while being focused and under control.

Be open to new ideas generated by the kids during the first stages of rehearsals. They will most likely come up with great ideas you never thought of, and the actors will feel personally invested in the production if their ideas are heard and, when possible, used. At a certain point, however, you need to establish the artistic decisions so that the play can be rehearsed with consistency and so that everyone can feel secure about it.

After casting and blocking, rehearse individual scenes while creating the production elements (sets, props, and costumes) which are added to rehearsals as they become available. If you don't have all the props available initially, use substitutes so that the actors can get used to them and where they belong. During this time the actors should be memorizing their lines, preferably at home.

The last few rehearsals should be run-throughs of the entire play. As you get close to the performance day, do a few run-throughs that are not interrupted and take notes which you can go over with the cast after the run-through. In addition to your notes, solicit the cast for their comments and suggestions about the run-through.

For one of your last, "dress" rehearsals, invite a preview audience. This will go a long way toward helping your actors focus their attention and get past some of their initial nervousness, as well as "jelling" the play production and working out the "bugs." At the end of this preview performance, ask the cast to sit on the stage while you solicit the audience's questions and comments. You will be amazed at how much a preview performance will improve your production.

If you feel your cast needs a little break from disciplined rehearsals, the following are some ideas for fun, alternative rehearsals, good for when morale is low:

- Rehearse the play in fast-forward. Not only is it extremely silly, it's a good way to drill the lines and blocking.
- Run the lines only, while everyone sits or lies down. A good drill.
- Do the play in gibberish, so that the actors must express their intent through tone of voice, facial expressions, and gestures. Also very silly.
- Switch roles. Seeing what other actors do with their roles can give actors new ideas. If they can't remember the lines exactly, they can paraphrase.

VOCAL PROJECTION

One of the biggest problems in producing plays with kids is getting them to speak loudly, slowly, and clearly. Be strict about vocal projection right from the start because if the audience can't understand the words the whole play will be lost on them.

Help the actors understand that speaking from the stage is not like normal speaking, that it must be louder, slower, and more clearly enunciated. The following are some activities for improving vocal projection:

- Pick a word or phrase from the script and have the actors stand and pretend to put those words in their hands. On the count of 1-2-3, say the words together while pantomiming "throwing" those words across the room and bouncing them off the far wall, as if throwing a ball.
- Practice breathing and good breath control at the beginning of every rehearsal. The diaphragm is a membrane below the lungs which supports good, deep breathing. Show the actors where their diaphragms are located (below the lungs and just above their stomachs) and with your hands on your diaphragms, together practice deep breathing while making your bellies go out on the inhale (the opposite of what

we're used to, which is bellies suck in on the inhale). Together repeat "Ho! Ho! Ho!" or "Sss! Sss! Sss!" while making your bellies jump outward on each syllable, to develop muscle control and awareness of the diaphragm.

• Do diction exercises. Here's a few drills (repeat each one over and over):
Topeka
Yamaha
Mama-le, Papa-le
But-a, gut-a
Red leather, yellow leather
B-B-B, B-B-B, BAH! *(and so forth through all the consonants of the alphabet)*
Slippery, southern snakes
Fresh fish, fried fish
You know you need unique New York.

PHYSICAL WARM-UPS

Besides vocal warm-ups, rehearsals should begin with some exercises to loosen up the body, for actors use their whole bodies, not just their voices, to express their characters. A regular discipline of warm-ups helps to focus attention and shift the mood of the group to one of rehearsal concentration. Warm-ups can include stretching, Hatha Yoga postures, and body awareness exercises, such as breathing into each body part, one at a time, and exhaling tension. Always include facial exercises (tongue warm-ups are always a hit).

OTHER EXERCISES & GAMES

When time permits, acting exercises and theater games can augment your rehearsals and help develop skills. They also contribute to a good spirit of group cooperation and add fun to rehearsals. The following are a few ideas:

• One person pantomimes a word, feeling, animal, household task, sport, or other activity while the rest of the group tries to figure out what it is. One variation is to have several ideas under the selected topic written on cards which the actors pick randomly.

- The entire group pantomimes an action, feeling, or sound. The director calls out what it is and the group silently acts it out. This exercise demonstrates that expression is not limited to sound or words.

- All stand in a circle while, one at a time, each person steps into the center, says his name while doing a movement, then steps back into the circle. The whole group together then repeats the name while making the same movement. This is a good activity for learning everyone's names and requires attention in order to mirror each person.

- Get in pairs, each couple facing each other and taking turns doing slow movements while their partner mirrors them. One variation is the director comes around and tries to figure out who is the originator of the movement and who is the mirror, or the whole group can witness each pair and try to figure out who is the originator and who is the mirror. Mirroring is a good exercise for focusing attention.

- All stand in a circle and one person begins by turning her head to the person on the right and saying a word. That person then turns to the person on the right and repeats the word and it continues thus, each person turning to the left to receive the word and to the right to send the word as it goes all around the circle. One variation is to have the director start a second word traveling in the opposite direction.

- All stand in a circle with their eyes closed and hold hands. One person begins to "pass the pulse" by gently squeezing the hand of the person on one side of them. That person continues to pass it and it goes around the circle. One variation is to add a second pulse going the opposite direction. The chief temptation is to start an illegitimate pulse, but if everyone cooperates this exercise can bring the group energy into focus.

- Stand or sit in a circle. The first person tosses a bean bag or rolls a ball to another person anywhere in the circle. That person then tosses it to another person and so forth while everyone keeps track of the order, each person receiving and giving it only once until it makes a complete circuit back to the first person. Continue to repeat this same pattern while adding a second and possibly a third bean bag or ball so that everyone has to stay totally alert at all times.

CHARACTERIZATION

The following are some ideas of ways to encourage the actors to develop their characters:

- From time to time, ask the actors what their character is thinking about or what they want to have happen at that moment in the story.
- Create a mock television interview show and invite each character, one at a time, to the stage to be interviewed by you, the television host, asking them questions about their character, their relationships to other characters, and their actions and intents in the story.
- Improvise scenes between the characters that are not in the play.
- Have the actors write mini-autobiographies of their characters.

MOVEMENT

The following are some ideas of movement activities that can enhance your rehearsals:

- Together as a group, move across the floor as the various characters would move. Ask the actors for words, verbs and adverbs, that describe the movements of each of the characters and all move to express those words.
- One at a time, actors can move across the room as their own character or another actor's character while the group watches and then copies. Actors can get new ideas for their characters by watching other actors move as their character. One variation is for each actor to not say which character is being expressed so that the group has to figure it out by examining the movement.
- Collaborate with a movement teacher who can work with the cast on movement skills and possible choreograph a dance for your show.

CURTAIN CALL & POST-PLAY DISCUSSION

Each actor should be able to take a bow by themselves, perhaps with their name and character announced, to receive their well-deserved applause. Any non-acting stage crew members can also be acknowledged and in the end, the entire cast and crew can take a bow together. Rehearse the bows and maintain onstage quiet and dignity throughout the curtain call, so that everyone gets respect and attention.

After the curtain call, the cast can sit on the stage for a post-play discussion with the audience. The director solicits questions and comments from the audience and facilitates the actors' answers. The actors like to show off and be the experts at this time: Both the curtain call and the post-play discussion are good self-esteem builders.

It's nice to then end the performance with a reception, or "cast party," with snacks and beverages, when the audience and cast can intermingle.

PRODUCTION

The following are some general guidelines for creating all the production elements (sets, props, costumes, and so on):

- Be creative with your resources—you don't have to spend a lot of money on materials. Paper, cardboard, markers, duct tape, and large fabric pieces can take care of most of your needs.
- Duct tape is your best friend—you can even find it in colors other than silver.
- Use the production tasks as activities in creating thinking. While giving the actors practical advice on how to make things, allow them to figure things out and come up with their own ideas for construction and design.
- Prepare each task to be as self-directed as possible. If you thoroughly prepare the materials the actors can work independently and this will free you from the stress of trying to help several groups make things at the same time, or allow you to rehearse with another group simultaneously.
- The directions for making sets, props, costumes, sound, and music listed in the appendixes for each script are only my suggestions—feel free to use other ideas for creating your own, unique production.
- Sets should be simple and light enough for the cast or crew to move themselves. Assign who is to move which set and when and rehearse all the set moves with the rest of the play.
- Props are not toys and should not be played with. They should only be handled by the actor who uses them. These are very important

rules! A missing or broken prop can be devastating in the middle of the play. Have the actors place their own props so they know where they are and always rehearse with props or prop substitutes.

- Create a structure for keeping the props in order backstage (otherwise, kids are often messy with them). Props tables, hooks on the wall, and exact places for each prop are extremely useful and much advised in order to avoid backstage havoc.
- Costumes need not be ornate. The best costumes are often those that the actors create themselves, with colored scarves or other costume props. Plain, black pants and shirts can be embellished with costume pieces that suggest the character, such as a hat, or animals ears and tail.
- If parents sew elaborate costumes they should make them for all the actors so that no child feels outshined. (I personally prefer kid-made costumes.)
- Makeup can be fun but should be optional, for not all children want to wear it. Eye shadow, rouge, and lipstick are easy to get and help bring out the actor's features. Eyebrow pencils are great for mustaches, evil eyebrows, and wicked scars.
- Some children may be allergic to makeup and sharing eye makeup can potentially spread eye diseases such as conjuctivitis (pink eye.) The safest bet is to have actors come with make-up already applied at home.
- "Lights" can be as simple as the switch on the wall. Flicking the lights off and on creates special effects. Table lamps, floor lamps, flashlights, and other lights can be used to create dramatic effects.
- Sound effects can be made with just about anything: percussion instuments, noisemakers, pots and pans...be creative! Tape players can provide music during scene changes which smoothes over the awkward silence while sets are being changed and gives your overall production a classy look.
- Music for songs or dances can be played on tape or CD or played live. If you have time and resources, such as a music teacher, you can create a music ensemble with some of the kids—a "pit orchestra"—to play sound effects and simple percussion.

Preface

I am Vi [taqʷšeblu] Hilbert, Upper Skagit elder, great-grandmother of four and Director of Lushootseed Research.

Because I am the only child of traditional Skagit historians, it has become my responsibility to pass on everything that my culture has taught me to pass on to coming generations of our "first people" (the natives of this country) and to all others who live among us on this land and on this earth.

The old stories of my people were used as our textbooks. They were told to guide us in practicing our age-old values, our history, our geography, our humor, and our memorization (because we had no written languages).

Our historians, those who were willing to have their voices recorded, left valuable information for us in our ancient Lushootseed (Puget Sound Salish) language. Because I have been fortunate enough to learn a writing system for this language, I have been able to bring their words to the printed page in both languages, Lushootseed and in translation to English. Lushootseed Press which I started in 1995 has published these volumes called *gʷəgʷulč̓e?*—Aunt Susie Sampson Peter and *siastenu?*—Gram Ruth Sehome Shelton. I have also done several other books, two of them were published by the University of Washington Press: an updated *Dictionary of Puget Sound Salish* (1994) and *Haboo*—a book of our literature (1985). In 1980 I self-published another book of our literature also titled *Haboo*. Each of these books contain 33 different stories.

These were textbooks that I used when I taught courses at the University of Washington, 1972–1987. Hundreds of students shared time with me in the classroom. They were from all over the country and there were some exchange students enrolled also from Germany and other countries. We learned from each other!

As an educator and great-grandmother, I feel it is part of my responsibility to accept invitations to lecture to all ages—preschool to senior citizens. It has been gratifying to share information from my culture with international groups also in Europe, Canada, Hawaii and South America.

In London, I was one of forty of the world's recognized storytellers. It was a revelation to some that the oral traditions of our world are indeed the common denominator. We see through our old stories how our wise ancestors taught in parallel fashions.

Pamela Gerke, in using two of the Lushootseed Epic stories to engage very young children in staging productions from another culture, proved to me that the power of our ancient stories can forever be used by all ages and cultures to meet human needs that fulfill those requirements that nurture the spirit of man!

—Vi [taqʷšeblu] Hilbert

CHAT BOTTÉ
Puss-In-Boots
(France)

This retelling of *Puss-In-Boots* is adapted from the work of Charles Perrault, the 17th century French author who published many fairy tales. It is Perrault's versions of such famous stories as *Cinderella* with which we are familiar. Due to his work, Perrault is in the same league as the Grimm Brothers of Germany and P.C. Asbjornsen and Jorgen E. Moe of Scandinavia, all of whom immortalized folktales by publishing popular versions of them.

The invention of the printing process forever altered the legacy of folktales by capturing in print that which until then had only been passed down orally from generation to generation. The versions of the tales we know are steeped in the social, cultural, philosophical, and political customs of the times and places in which they were originally set to print. Today, movies, television, and computers are providing us with new ways to retell and interact with folktales, which are, likewise, influenced by and reflective of modern culture. Look for the golden thread of *the story* which survives all of these changes of venue and time period.

In *Chat Botté,* it's obvious that the cat is indeed the master of his human owner. In folktales, animals often portray magical reality that is beyond reason but which brings good fortune. In this story, youngest Enfant obeys his magical cat and is rewarded with wealth, prestige, and true love in much the same way that the Young Archer of *The Firebird, the Horse of Power and Czarevna Vasilisa* is saved by the advice of his Horse of Power. (See volume I of this series.)

This production includes the possibility of creating a large Ogre puppet, if you have the time and resources for a big art project. There's also a french folksong included for an optional song and/or dance.

RUNNING TIME OF THE SHOW *(approximate)*:
20 minutes
REHEARSAL TIME NEEDED:
7-10 hours
OTHER PRODUCTION TIME NEEDED:
2-3 hours
CAST SIZE:
Minimum: 7, plus Narrator (Miller, Oldest Enfant and Second Enfant can all double as other characters after Scene 1; Servants can double as Haymakers; Courtiers, Rabbit, and Duck can be eliminated; Ogre can also play Lion and Mouse.)

Maximum: 20-25 (Servants, Haymakers, and Courtiers can each be played by small groups; Rabbit and Duck can be played by actors rather than stuffed animals; Lion and Mouse can be played by two separate actors, in addition to the Ogre)
GENDER OF CHARACTERS:
To be true to the tradition of this story, the Miller is a man with three sons, the youngest of whom encounters a King and marries a Princess. However, if the gender of the main characters is reversed, I think the story works just as well. Chat, the Ogre, Servants, Haymakers, and Courtiers can be played as female and/or male. Note the male/female differences in the French vocabulary list in Appendix A and alter the text accordingly.

CHARACTERS:
NARRATOR
CHAT BOTTÉ – Puss-In-Boots, a clever cat
MILLER
ELDEST ENFANT – the Miller's oldest child
SECOND ENFANT – the Miller's middle child
YOUNGEST ENFANT – the Miller's youngest child
RABBIT (optional – can be played by a stuffed animal)
DUCK (optional – can be played by a stuffed animal)
LE ROI (or LA REINE) – the King (or Queen)
LA PRINCESSE (or LE PRINCE) – daughter (or son) of the King
   (or Queen)
SERVANT #1
SERVANT #2
OTHER SERVANTS (optional)
COURTIERS (optional) – ladies and gentlemen of the royal court
HAYMAKERS – local peasants
OGRE – a wicked, magical giant (can be played by a large puppet)
LION (optional – can be played by the Ogre)
MOUSE (optional – can be played by the Ogre or a windup mouse)

SCENE 1

(Setting: The countryside of France, in the days of French royalty. In one area of the stage is the cottage of the Miller, including one chair and possibly an interior wall. In another area of the stage is a pond made of blue fabric. Nearby is a bush. There may also be a backdrop of the countryside on the upstage wall. LIGHTS UP.)

NARRATOR: Long ago in France there lived a Miller.

(MILLER enters and sits in chair.)

NARRATOR: When he became very old, he asked his three children, *trois enfants*, to come to him.

(ELDEST, SECOND & YOUNGEST ENFANTS enter and stand around MILLER.)

MILLER: Oldest *Enfant*, you shall inherit my mill.
ELDEST: *Merci beaucoup, Papa!*

(ELDEST exits.)

MILLER: Second *Enfant*, you shall inherit my donkey.
SECOND: *Merci beaucoup, Papa!*

(SECOND exits.)

MILLER: And to you, my Youngest *Enfant*, I shall leave my cat, *mon chat.*

(CHAT BOTTÉ enters and dances around.)

YOUNGEST: *(Disappointed.) Merci Beaucoup, Papa.*

(MILLER exits. YOUNGEST sits in the chair, sadly.)

YOUNGEST: My brothers can use the mill and the donkey to work together. But how can I make a living with just this *chat*?
CHAT: Cheer up! Have a pair of boots made for me so that I can run through the sharp brambles! And get me a big sack!
YOUNGEST: *(Shocked and delighted.) Oui! Oui!*

(YOUNGEST exits and returns with a big sack and a pair of red boots which he gives to CHAT. CHAT may also put on a cape and a

hat with a large feather in it at this time. CHAT puts on the boots and admires himself.)

CHAT: I am now *Chat Botté*, Puss-In-Boots!

NARRATOR: *Chat Botté* now told the Miller's son to get her lettuce and carrots.

(YOUNGEST exits and returns with lettuce and carrots which CHAT puts in the sack.)

NARRATOR: *Chat Botté* now went to where many wild rabbits lived.

(CHAT goes to the bush while YOUNGEST exits. CHAT crouches by the bush, holding the sack open.)

NARRATOR: She waited for a foolish young rabbit to come along.

(RABBIT enters – can be a stuffed rabbit pushed through an opening in the bush. CHAT pounces on it.)

CHAT: MRRROW!!!

(She puts the sack around the RABBIT and exits.)

NARRATOR: *Chat Botté* carried the rabbit to the palace of the King, *Le Roi.*

(LIGHTS DOWN. Change set: remove Miller's cottage and replace with palace.)

SCENE 2

(Setting: Palace of Le Roi, including two thrones and possibly an interior wall. Palace door can be pantomimed but there is some sort of doorbell. Pond and bush remain as is in another area of the stage. LE ROI & LA PRINCESSE enter and sit on thrones. SERVANTS & COURTIERS enter and stand about the palace. LIGHTS UP. CHAT enters and goes to palace door, rings bell. SERVANTS answer.)

CHAT: *Bonjour!*
SERVANTS: *Bonjour, mademoiselle!*
CHAT: I would like to speak with *Le Roi, s'il vous plâit.*
SERVANTS: *Oui, mademoiselle!*

(SERVANTS bring CHAT to LE ROI. CHAT bows low, then takes the RABBIT out of the sack.)

CHAT: My master, *Le Marquis de Carabas,* sends this gift to you!
LE ROI & LA PRINCESSE: *Merci beaucoup!*
LA PRINCESSE: Papa, who is *Le Marquis de Carabas?*
LE ROI: I've never heard of him! *(To CHAT:)* I gladly accept his gift.

(A SERVANT takes RABBIT and exits with it.)

COURTIERS & SERVANTS: *(Whispering to each other.)* Who is *Le Marquis de Carabas?*
CHAT: *Au revoir!*
ALL: *Au revoir!*

(CHAT bows and exits. LIGHTS DOWN.)

SCENE 3

(Setting: The same. All in palace remain as is. DUCK enters and sits on pond. LIGHTS UP.)

NARRATOR: The next day *Chat Botté* went back to the pond near the Miller's house.

(CHAT enters with sack, goes to pond and crouches at the edge of it, holding the sack open.)

NARRATOR: She had filled the sack with grain and now she waited for a foolish young duck to come along.

(CHAT pounces on the DUCK.)

CHAT: MRRROW!!!

(She puts the sack around the DUCK. She goes to the palace door and rings the bell. SERVANTS answer.)

CHAT: *Bonjour!*
SERVANTS: *Bonjour, mademoiselle!*
CHAT: I would like to speak with *Le Roi, s'il vous plâit.*
SERVANTS: *Oui, mademoiselle!*

(SERVANTS bring CHAT to LE ROI. CHAT bows low, then takes the DUCK out of the sack.)

CHAT: My master, *Le Marquis de Carabas,* sends this duck to you!
LE ROI & LA PRINCESSE: *Merci beaucoup!*

(A SERVANT takes DUCK and exits with it.)

COURTIERS & SERVANTS: *(whispering to each other)* Who is *Le Marquis de Carabas?*
CHAT: *Au revoir!*
ALL: *Au revoir!*

(CHAT bows and exits. LIGHTS DOWN.)

SCENE 4

(Setting: The same. ALL in palace remain as is. LIGHTS UP. CHAT enters and stands where she can eavesdrop on the SERVANTS.)

NARRATOR: Chat Botté continued to bring gifts to *Le Roi* for the next two or three months. One day, she overheard two servants talking.
SERVANT #1: Today *Le Roi* will go for a drive along the river!
SERVANT #2: And he'll take his daughter, *La Princesse,* with him!
NARRATOR When she heard this, *Chat Botté* hurried back to her master.

(CHAT runs back to the pond as YOUNGEST ENFANT enters there.)

CHAT: Your fortune will be made today! All you have to do is go for a swim in the pond. Leave the rest to me!
YOUNGEST: *Oui!*

(YOUNGEST takes off jacket and gets "into" the pond by laying underneath the fabric. CHAT stashes the jacket in the bushes. Meanwhile, LE ROI & LA PRINCESSE get into their carriage, a decorated wagon pulled by SERVANTS and attended by COURTIERS.)

NARRATOR: Soon the carriage of *Le Roi* and *La Princesse* passed by.

(LE ROI'S carriage approaches the pond. CHAT runs toward them.)

CHAT: *Au secours! Au secours!* Help! Help! *Le Marquis de Carabas* has been robbed of his clothes!

COURTIERS & SERVANTS: *Mon Dieu!*

LE ROI: Servants! Run back to the palace and bring some of my finest clothes!

SERVANTS: *Oui!*

(SERVANTS run back to the palace for clothes.)

YOUNGEST: *(Whispering to CHAT.)* Who is *Le Marquis de Carabas?*

CHAT: It's you, stupid!

(SERVANTS return with a royal jacket which they give to YOUNGEST. He puts it on while CHAT slips away, unnoticed.)

LE ROI: Come for a ride with me and my daughter!

YOUNGEST: *Merci beaucoup!*

(YOUNGEST gets into the carriage and they exit. LIGHTS DOWN. Change set: Remove palace, bush and pond and replace with hayfield and Ogre's castle.)

SCENE 5

(Setting: Hayfield is in one area of the stage, Ogre's castle is in another area. Hayfield is indicated by a freestanding wall of hayfield landscape. Ogre's castle includes a freestanding interior wall. If you use a windup mouse, there should be a small opening along the bottom of the wall for it to come through. Behind the wall is a stool for the Ogre to stand on so that he appears to loom large over the top of the wall. OGRE can also be played by a large puppet. OGRE is hidden behind the wall when the scene opens. Near the entrance to the castle hangs a sign that reads: "Chez d'Ogre." Backstage is a table set for a feast. HAYMAKERS enter and work in the field. LIGHTS UP.)

NARRATOR: Meanwhile, *Chat Botté* ran ahead to where some workers were cutting hay in a field. She told them that when *Le Roi* passed by, they were to tell him that their hayfield belonged to *Le Marquis de Carabas.*

CHAT: And if you don't I shall chop you fine as mincemeat!

HAYMAKERS: *(Afraid.) Oui!*

(CHAT exits, running. LE ROI and his entourage enter in the carriage. When they pass by the hayfield, they stop.)

LE ROI: *(Calling out.)* To whom does this fine hayfield belong?
HAYMAKERS: *Le Marquis de Carabas!*

(LE ROI is obviously impressed and they exit. HAYMAKERS exit.)

NARRATOR: *Chat Botté* raced on ahead, ordering all the field-workers to tell *Le Roi* that their lands belonged to *Le Marquis de Carabas*. The workers, intimidated by this fearsome chat, did as they were told and thus *Le Roi* was more and more impressed with the great wealth of *Le Marquis*. After awhile, *Chat Botté* came to a stately castle which belonged to a wicked ogre, a giant who possessed magical powers.

(CHAT enters and goes up to castle and knocks. OGRE stands up on stool behind wall, presenting a very grotesque image.)

OGRE: WHAT DO YOU WANT?!!!
CHAT: I have come to pay my respects to the great Ogre!
OGRE: SINCE YOU PUT IT THAT WAY, COME ON IN!!!

(CHAT enters castle and bows before the OGRE.)

CHAT: *Bonjour, monsieur!* Is it true that you have such great powers that you can turn yourself into a lion?
OGRE: *OUI!!!*

(OGRE ducks down behind wall. SOUND & LIGHTS effects. LION comes charging out.)

LION: RROOAARR!!!
CHAT: *Mon Dieu!*

(LION chases CHAT around the castle, but CHAT manages to escape.)

CHAT: *(To LION.)* A lion is easy – can you also turn yourself into something very small, like a mouse?
LION: *OUI!!!*

(LION goes behind the wall. SOUND & LIGHTS effects. MOUSE comes out from behind wall. CHAT pounces on it.)

CHAT: MRRROW!!!

(CHAT gleefully holds MOUSE by holding it's tail in her teeth. Just then, LE ROI and his entourage arrive in their carriage.)

SERVANTS: Prepare for the arrival of his majesty, *Le Roi!*

CHAT: *Mon Dieu!*

(She quickly disposes of the MOUSE, then goes to castle entrance.)

CHAT: Welcome to the castle of *Le Marquis de Carabas!* *(Bows.)*

PRINCESSE: *C'est tres belle!*

NARRATOR: *Chat Botté* brought them all into the castle where a magnificent feast had been prepared.

(SERVANTS get the feast table and bring it on-stage.)

NARRATOR: While they were feasting, *Le Marquis de Carabas* asked *La Princesse* to marry him.

PRINCESSE: *Oui!*

NARRATOR: There was much merrymaking that day. *Chat Botté* led all the dances.

(May have song/dance here: "Il Court, Il Court Le Furet" or other song.)

ALL: *C'est fini!* The end!

APPENDIX A: VOCABULARY LIST
OF FOREIGN LANGUAGE

FRENCH	ENGLISH	PRONUNCIATION
au revoir	good-bye	oh reh-vwah'
au secours!	help!	oh seh-koor'
bonjour	good day, hello	bohn-jhoor'
c'est fini	it is finished, the end	say fin-ee'
c'est très belle	it is beautiful	say tray' bell
chat, Chat Botté	cat, "Puss-In-Boots" ("the booted cat")	shah, shah bo-tay'
enfant / trois enfants	child / 3 children	ahn-fahn' / twahz ahn-fahn' *
Le Marquis de Carabas	the Marquis of Carabas (male)	luh mar-keez' duh kuh-rah'-bahs
La Marquise	the Marquise (female)	lah mar-keez'-uh
la princesse le prince	the princess the prince	lah prahn-seh' + luh prahns *
le roi / la reine	the king / the queen	luh r'wah / lah rehne +
mademoiselle / monsieur	miss / mister	ma-dem-mwah-zell' / muss-yeur'
merci beaucoup	thank you very much	mehr-see' bow-koo'
mon Dieu!	my God!	mohn d'yeuh' *
oui	yes	wee
s'il vous plâit	please	see voo play'

"Il Court, Il Court Le Furet" (song):

Il court, il court le furet	he runs, he runs, the weasel	eel koor', eel koor' luh fuh-ray'
Le furet du bois mesdames	the weasel through the forest, ladies	luh fuh-ray' doo bwah' may-dahm'
Le furet du bois joli	the weasel through the pretty forest	luh fuh-ray' doo bwah' jho-lee'
Il a passé par ici	he passes by here	eel ah pah'-say par ee-see'

* French "n" is sounded in the back of the throat
+ French "r" is sounded in the back of the throat, gutterally

SETS LIST

MILLER'S COTTAGE:
    1 chair
    interior, freestanding wall (optional)

COUNTRYSIDE:
    Pond (blue fabric laid on the floor)
    Bush (freestanding wall; hayfield on the back)

PALACE:
    2 thrones
    interior, freestanding wall (Ogre's palace on the back)

HAYFIELD:
    backdrop on freestanding wall (bush on the back)

OGRE'S CASTLE:
    interior, freestanding wall (palace on the back)
    1 stool or chair
    table

OPTIONAL:
    landscape backdrop

HOW TO MAKE THE SETS

FREESTANDING WALLS (for Miller's cottage, bush/hayfield, palace/Ogre's castle)
- very large, cardboard box
- cardboard cutting knife
- scissors
- heavy butcher paper
- tape or glue
- markers, crayons or paint with brushes
- colored paper or fabric (optional)

Cut box to create a freestanding wall with accordion folds. If you are using a stuffed animal rabbit, the bush can have a hatch cut into the middle of it for passing it through. If you are using a windup mouse, Ogre's castle wall can have a small opening along the bottom for passing it through. To cut hatches, draw a square on the cardboard, large enough for the intended objects. Cut sides and bottom of square and fold up top to create a hatch door. Cut two pieces of butcher paper to size of the wall. Tape or glue paper to both sides of the wall, including any hatches (if cardboard is plain white, you can eliminate this step). Draw picture of the set on the wall with markers, crayons or paint. Colored paper or fabric can also be used to decorate the wall, using glue or tape.

THRONES
- 2 chairs
- large fabric pieces
- sturdy tape
- junk jewelry
- safety pins

Drape the chairs with fabric. Tape securely on back and bottom of chairs. Pin jewelry along the top and sides of the chairs.

LANDSCAPE BACKDROP
- heavy butcher paper
- markers, crayons or paint with brushes
- sturdy tape
- scissors

Cut butcher paper to fit across upstage wall. Draw scenes of the French countryside with markers, crayons or paint. Make sure the artists understand which end is up and that drawings must be large enough to be seen from the audience. Tape to wall.

APPENDIX C: PROPS

PROPS LIST

Boots (see Costumes, Chat)
Large Sack
Lettuce & Carrots
Stuffed Animal Rabbit (optional)
Stuffed Animal Duck (optional)
Royal Carriage
Hat Sickles
Windup Mouse(optional)
Food & Drink (bottles, bowls, and so forth.)

HOW TO MAKE THE PROPS

LARGE SACK
- large piece of fabric
- sewing machine or stapler
- scissors
- short length or rope

If you have actors playing the Rabbit and the Duck, the sack must be large enough to fit over both actors and cut open at the bottom. Sew or staple the sack out of fabric which is thin enough to see through, or cut eye holes for the actor inside. Sew or staple a length of rope near the top which can be wrapped around the top of the sack and tied. Chat Botté pulls the sack over the actor's head and secures the tie at the top, and the actor in the sack simply walks.

LETTUCE & CARROTS

Use the real thing or plastic objects, or fashion out of cardboard and colored paper or papier mâché.

ROYAL CARRIAGE
- child's pull wagon, large enough for three children
- large cardboard pieces
- cardboard cutting tool
- sturdy tape
- colored paper
- scissors
- glitter
- glue
- markers, crayons, or paint with brushes

Cut cardboard to represent the sides of the carriage. Decorate with colored paper, markers, crayons, paint and/or glitter. Tape securely to sides of the wagon, making sure that the actors can still fit inside. Servants pull/push the wagon.

HAY SICKLES
- long dowels or other rods
- sturdy cardboard pieces
- cardboard cutting tool
- compass (circle drawing tool)
- sturdy tape
- markers, crayons or paint with brushes (as needed)

Using the compass, draw an arc on a cardboard piece from which you can then draw a semicircle, about 6-8 cm wide, pointed on one end and wide on the other end. Cut out and color as needed. Tape the wide end to the top of a dowel or rod.

COSTUMES LIST

MILLER & ELDEST & SECOND SONS / DAUGHTERS: plain, working-class clothes of the time period

YOUNGEST: same as the above but must include a jacket or dress which can be easily taken off, with plain, dark clothing underneath

A royal-looking jacket or dress which can be easily put on

CHAT BOTTÉ: elegant pants and shirt, may include a vest, plus red or other bright boots, ears and tail

Optional: a fabulous hat with a large, sweeping feather; a cape

ALL ROYALTY: royal-type clothing of the time period, with crowns and junk jewelry

COURTIERS: rich-looking clothing of the time period

SERVANTS & HAYMAKERS: poor, peasant clothes; may include aprons

OGRE: grotesque costume; possibly including a mask, or the entire Ogre can be a large puppet

LION & MOUSE: plain, dark or colored clothing, with ears and tail

HOW TO MAKE THE COSTUMES

ANIMAL EARS
- colored construction paper
- pencil
- scissors
- stapler
- light cardboard, glue (optional)
- markers, crayons, paint with brushes, (optional)
- fake fur, glue (optional)

Draw and cut out shape of animal ears with pencil on appropriate color of paper. Cut long strips of the same colors, approximately 4 cm wide and long enough to go around the actors' heads with 2-3 centimeters of overlap. Staple ears to strips and staple strips to fit snugly around the actors' heads. You may want to reinforce ears and strips with a cardboard backing. Decorate as needed with markers, crayons, paint or bits of fake fur.

ANIMAL TAILS
for Chat Botté, Lion, and Mouse:
- long strips, approx. 1 meter long, of colored chiffon or other light fabric
- scissors
- long, elastic strip or safety pins

Measure out three strips of fabric. Braid together and tie in a knot at either end. Tail is either pinned to back of actor's pants or tied to an elastic strip that is measured and tied to fit around actor's waist. The best place to pin the tail to pants is through belt loops. If you pin it directly to pants or shirt, it can rip the fabric if someone steps on the tail.

for Rabbit:
- big puff ball (try a craft supply store)
- safety pin

for Duck:
- feathers
- tape
- long, elastic strip

Measure and tie the elastic to fit around the actor's waist. Tape the feathers to the back of the elastic. You can also do a similar thing around the actor's head.

CROWNS
- shiny, gold paper or cardboard
- scissors
- glue
- fake jewels

Draw the crown shape, flat, on the gold paper or cardboard. If using paper, measure and cut a piece of light cardboard to reinforce it and glue it on the back. Glue jewels to the crown and allow time to dry. Cut a strip of the gold paper or cardboard 5 cm wide and staple to the side of the crown, measuring the whole to fit around the actor's head.

OGRE MASK OR PUPPET
Use any mask-making or puppet-making technique to create a fearsome character.

SOUND:

Door knock or doorbell: wood blocks or bells

Magic of Ogre changing shape: percussion instruments, bells, and so on.

MUSIC:

"Il Court, Il Court Le Furet" or other French folksong (optional):

Note: You can change the words *"Le Furet"* to *"Chat Botté"*.

French music to play during scene changes, on CD, tape or played live

IL COURT, IL COURT LE FURET
("The Weasel Runs, Runs")

DA-HOOS-WHEE'-WHEE
"The Seal-Hunting Brothers"
(Lushootseed Salish)

This story comes from the Lushootseed Salish, the Native American or "First People" of the Puget Sound region of Western Washington, near Seattle. The Lushootseed have a rich oral tradition which has only been put into written form in the last few decades. This script is adapted from a telling by Martha LaMont at Tulalip, Washington, in 1966. Her exact wording has been preserved, except for a few slight changes for the sake of clarity or brevity.

I was fortunate to have received approval for adapting some Lushootseed tales to play format from Vi Hilbert, translator and editor of much of Lushootseed oral tradition (see Volume I of this series for another Lushootseed play, *Star Story.*) All teachers in search of multicultural experiences for their students must be sensitive to the issues around "cultural appropriation"—when people of the dominant (white) culture use the traditions of people of other cultures, without permission. Always take care to seek education from authentic resources (people, books, and so on) of the culture being studied.

There are many tribes in the Puget Sound region, each with their own language and traditions. It's a common mistake to lump together many different Native American tribes as if they were all the same. The Lushootseed Salish words and story in this play are specifically from the area north of the present Snohomish-King County line, just north of Seattle.

I've also included a short write-up about Lushootseed Salish culture, Appendix F. Whereas the other cultures and countries represented in this book can most likely be researched at local libraries, information on Lushootseed Salish culture may prove difficult or impossible to find (even in Seattle).

This story tells of the epic journey of two intrepid brothers who are bewitched by the evil grandfather of their sister's husband. The brothers go on a "spirit journey" into the unknown and come back home empowered by their experience, singing their "spirit songs."

A "spirit journey" is when a person goes on a journey of self-discovery and comes back with the wisdom of self-knowledge or spiritual insight. Spirit journeys are respected in the culture of the First People and many are recorded as stories. The other Lushootseed tale in this volume, *Legend of the Seasons,* is also a metaphorical spirit journey.

"Spirit songs" are personal songs which are given to each person by spiritual powers, and the singing of a person's own spirit songs brings them strength and energy. The songs included for the Lushootseed stories in this collection reportedly have an origin in Native American songs but have been altered and adapted by the dominant (white) culture over many years and many campfires. They are offered here with respect for true Native American songs and without the intention of imitating such.

RUNNING TIME OF SHOW: *(approximate)*
25-30 minutes
REHEARSAL TIME NEEDED:
12-15 hours
OTHER PRODUCTION TIME NEEDED:
4-6 hours
CAST SIZE:
    Minimum: 10, plus Narrator (Except for Da-Hoos-Whee'-Whee, all other actors can play more than one role. The Dwarf's lines can be consolidated.)
    Maximum: 30-35
GENDER OF CHARACTERS:
    Soup'kss, Dwarves, Hot'-hot, Chuh-hoo-loo' and Villagers can be played as either female or male; all other characters should be played as designated.

CHARACTERS:
    NARRATOR
    DA-HOOS-WHEE'-WHEE:
        OLDER BROTHER
        YOUNGER BROTHER
    SISTER – of the Brothers
    MAN – husband of their Sister
    CHILDREN – of Sister and Man
    TSAH'-PAH – grandfather of Man
    MAN'S BROTHERS
    SOUP'-KSS – seal
    DWARVES
    OLD MAN DWARF
    HOT'-HOT – ducks
    HOT'-HOT SIAB – Head Man of the ducks
    KAI'-YAH – grandmother of Seal-Hunting Brothers
    CHUH-HOO-LOO' – whale
    LITTLE BROTHER – of Seal-Hunting Brothers
    STEPMOTHER – of Little Brother
    BAHD – father of Seal-Hunting Brothers and Little Brother
    YOUNG WOMAN
    SPIRIT POWERS (optional):
        DEER
        SMELT
        BEAR
        OTHER GAME

SCENE 1

(Setting: A Lushootseed village on Puget Sound, long ago. There are two-three large, sturdy tables upstage which will be longhouses for both the Lushootseed village and the village of the DWARVES. The facade of each house may either be cloth hanging from the tabletops to the floor, downstage, or freestanding cardboard walls set in front of the tables. Behind the tables, upstage, are chairs or other access to the tabletops for the HOT'-HOT in Scene 3. There is a fire pit set in front of the center longhouse. There is space downstage for the beach and the ocean. Some of the ocean scenes could take place in the aisles of the audience. The canoes can either be made using small, children's wagons or can be made of cardboard boxes with the bottoms cut out, propelled by the actors walking inside while holding up the sides with their hands. LIGHTS UP.)

NARRATOR: This is a story from the Lushootseed Salish of western Washington. The story begins in a village by the salt water of Puget Sound. These were the people who lived there: a man, his wife and his *Tsah'-pah*, his grandfather...

(MAN, SISTER & TSAH'-PAH enter one at a time as their names are called. MAN exits to one side while SISTER & TSAH'-PAH go into house, center.)

NARRATOR: ...And also her two young brothers, who were seal-hunters, *Da-hoos-whee'-whee*.

(DA-HOOS-WHEE'-WHEE enter, in canoe and during the following narration they get out of canoe and carry some fresh fish to their SISTER'S house.)

NARRATOR: These brothers were great hunters on land and on the water. When they hunted out on the salt water, they used their *tkl'-ai*, their canoe which they themselves had made.

(SISTER comes out of house and DA-HOOS-WHEE'-WHEE give her the fish. She takes it and goes back inside and they exit.)

NARRATOR: The brother-in-law of the hunters arrived.

(MAN enters as SISTER comes out of her house.)

MAN: *Tsi siab!* Hello!

SISTER: *Siab!*

MAN: Did your brothers give you any of the game that they got?

SISTER: *Whee!* No! They don't give us anything.

(MAN, angry, exits. During the following narration, DA-HOOS-WHEE'-WHEE enter and give SISTER more food which she takes inside her house and they exit.)

NARRATION: She has, however, been given food. Her brothers give her *soup'-kss*, seal, and porpoise and fish that they have already cooked for her. They expect her to set some aside for her husband to eat when he returns from his work.

(MAN enters as SISTER comes out of her house.)

MAN: *Tsi siab!*

SISTER: *Siab!*

MAN: Did your brothers give you any of the game that they got?

SISTER: *Whee!* No! They don't give us anything.

(MAN, angry, exits. CHILDREN come out of their house with platters of food and greedily gobble it all – pantomime.)

NARRATOR: Each time the brothers bring food for their sister and her family she and her children eat all of it. She never sets aside anything for her husband. She has her children sprinkle ashes from the fire on their wooden platters.

(They do so – pantomime.)

NARRATOR: She rubs their mouths with the ashes to hide any traces of grease from the food that they have eaten.

(She does so – pantomime.)

SISTER: Be very quiet and pretend to be hungry!

NARRATOR: Now the woman's husband gets very angry as he thinks about his hungry family.

(MAN enters.)

MAN: *Tsi siab!*

SISTER: *Siab!*

MAN: Your brothers, as usual, have not given you any food?

WOMAN: *Whee!* No! They don't give us anything. Just look at your children, they have had nothing to eat!

(CHILDREN whimper.)

WOMAN: The same is true for myself!

NARRATOR: However, she is full of food, this bad woman! Now the man became very angry and he talked to his brothers and *Tsah'-pah.*

(SISTER & CHILDREN go into house while MAN'S BROTHERS & TSAH'-PAH enter.)

MAN: What do you think about our killing our brothers-in-law, *Da-hoos-whee-whee?*

BROTHER #1: Just restrain yourself.

TSAH'-PAH: We shall just put a spell on them! You will pretend to see something way over on the other side of the harbor, and you will come and say to them, "There is a big *soup'-kss,* a seal way over there. You could sneak up on it, you are such good hunters!"

MAN & BROTHERS: *Aiii!* Yes!

(MAN'S BROTHERS & TSAH'-PAH exit while DA-HOOS-WHEE'-WHEE enter and MAN goes to them.)

NARRATOR: The woman's husband went to his brothers-in-law and spoke to them as the old man had told him to.

DA-HOOS-WHEE'-WHEE: *Aiii!* You don't have to say anymore, we're going! *Huy!*

(MAN exits as DA-HOOS-WHEE'-WHEE get into canoe and paddle out to sea while SOUP'-KSS enters, splashing in water and making seal noises.)

NARRATOR: They could see that there was indeed a great *soup'-kss* out on the water, bending backward and making noises as seals usually do. However, it was the work of the bad old man. He made the *soup'-kss* and instructed it to take *Da-hoos-whee'-whee* far across the ocean to the very edge. The young men went and harpooned the *soup'-kss.*

(OLDER BROTHER harpoons SOUP'-KSS – actor throws harpoon which the other actor catches and holds it, as if it has been speared.

MUSIC BEGINS: drums. SOUP'-KSS thrashes around while DA-HOOS-WHEE'-WHEE are tossed around in their canoe. DRUMS continue under the following.)

NARRATOR: They were thrown around as they tried to overcome it! Older Brother had hold of the line to his harpoon, which was in the *soup'-kss.* After they had gone quite a way he opened his hand to let go of the line. But he couldn't let go! His hand was stuck!

OLDER BROTHER: Maybe we have had a spell put on us by our brother-in-law's *Tsah'-pah!*

YOUNGER BROTHER: We'll let this *soup'-kss* take us wherever it will!

NARRATOR: Every now and then the *soup'-kss* would dive and surface again. It did this for many days.

(SOUP'-KSS exits followed by DA-HOOS-WHEE'-WHEE. LIGHTS DOWN. MUSIC ENDS.)

SCENE 2

(Setting: The shore near the village of the DWARVES, the next morning. LIGHTS UP. DA-HOOS-WHEE'-WHEE enter in canoe. Their harpoon is attached to a big log.)

NARRATOR: It was night when the *soup'-kss* arrived with them at a certain place. There was land nearby. They had been released! There floating in front of them was a great big log of cedar, *huh-pai',* covered with tangled roots and branches. The Older Brother began pulling at his harpoon line, and it took him right to the big, branchy, floating *huh-pai'* log.

(He does so.)

NARRATOR: So it had been this log which he had speared and that had been the thing which ran off with them when they came under the spell!

OLDER BROTHER: That evil old man put a spell on us, and that is why we are far away!

YOUNGER BROTHER: It seems we have been taken clear across the ocean. We had better lift up our *tkl'-ai* and hide it. Let's lie down behind it and be quiet.

OLDER BROTHER: *Aiii!*

(They beach their canoe and hide behind it.)

NARRATOR: There they were hiding when they saw a child come into view in a large *tkl'-ai*.

(DWARF #1 enters in a canoe. He acts out the following.)

NARRATOR: Suddenly he began to go to and fro from one end of the *tkl'-ai* to the other. Then he got down and he dove. He was there at the bottom of the ocean for some time. Suddenly he surfaced and he was holding several halibut.

(DWARF #1 puts halibut in his canoe. He acts out the following.)

NARRATOR: Again the child dove, emerging again with four halibut which he put into the *tkl'-ai*. The brothers' mouths were watering as they saw the good food that this creature was getting. They decided to help themselves to his halibut before he comes up from his dive.

(DA-HOOS-WHEE'-WHEE sneak over to DWARF #1's canoe, take the fish, return to their hiding place and hungrily eat the fish. DWARF #1 acts out the following.)

NARRATOR: The child emerged. He got into his *tkl'-ai* and missed the food which he had caught. Then this is what he did – he pointed toward the shore to where they were! They still think it is a child. However, this person is what people call a dwarf, an old one.

DWARF #1: *(Thinking aloud.)* I had better take these strange people who come from somewhere. And I shall also take their *tkl'-ai*.

(DWARF #1 goes to shore, grabs DA-HOOS-WHEE'-WHEE and puts them in his canoe. He ties their canoe to his own and, getting into their canoe, begins to paddle.)

NARRATOR: He had kidnapped them! They were wondering where they would be taken.

DWARF #1: Don't be afraid. One of our children will come for you.

NARRATOR: Now the two brothers knew that Dwarves had kidnapped them. They are grown adults yet they are small like children.

(ALL exit. LIGHTS DOWN. Change set: Change longhouse facades to colorful ones; bring out pile of shells.)

SCENE 3

(Setting: The village of the DWARVES, a few minutes later. The facades of the longhouses are very colorful and fanciful. Either colorful cloths are hung from the tabletops to the floor, downstage, or free-standing walls are turned around to show a colorful side. If using cloth for longhouse facades, colorful cloths can be pre-taped to downstage edge of tabletops, on top of the plainer cloths for the Lushootseed village longhouses. The colorful cloths can be folded back over the tabletops during the first two scenes, simply pulled to hang down in front for this scene, then folded back over the tabletops for the last scene. There is a fire pit in front of the center house – same as for Scene 1. There is a huge pile of dentalium shells near the shore, downstage. DWARVES enter and mill about the village. Some Hot'-Hot sits on rooftops. LIGHTS UP. DWARF #1 and DA-HOOS-WHEE'-WHEE enter, in canoes.)

NARRATOR: The Dwarf took them over the water around the point. The people who lived there were not the usual kind of people. Everything there was colored. There were lots of Dwarves walking around all over – little tiny people, yet they are grown-ups.

(DWARF #1 & DA-HOOS-WHEE'-WHEE beach their canoes. DA-HOOS-WHEE'-WHEE gape at the pile of shells.)

NARRATOR: The dentalia were piled high. This was their food. It was a shellfish which they could get when the tide was out. They also dove underwater to get this mollusk. They ate what was inside the shell. These shells were things which *Da-hoos-whee'-whee* prized. They thought they should try to sort out some of the larger ones to take with them if they could manage to be taken home. The Dwarf took them up from the shore to a place where there were longhouses clustered together.

(DWARF #1 leads DA-HOOS-WHEE'-WHEE to longhouses. They sit in front of the fire pit. DWARVES gather around to stare at them.)

OLD MAN: *(To Dwarves:)* Look at these people. They are really people, wherever it is that they come from. Get busy and prepare some food. It should just be some soup, because they're very weak now and their stomachs aren't very strong.

(Some DWARVES bring out bowls and give them to DA-HOOS-WHEE'-WHEE who eat out of them – pantomime.)

NARRATOR: After they had finished eating they were questioned about their own homeland. The brothers carefully explained what had happened to them.

OLD MAN: This is the land of the Dwarves where you have come.

DWARF #2: We can communicate with those salmon and *Hot'-hot,* ducks of all kinds. Our language is the same!

NARRATOR: The brothers looked longingly at the *Hot'-hot.* They enjoyed eating duck. Meanwhile, *Kai'-yah,* their grandmother, mourned for the lost brothers.

(ALL freeze. LIGHTS DOWN. LIGHTS UP on KAI'-YAH who stands off to one side, perhaps on a table.)

NARRATOR: She mourned the loss of *Da-hoos-whee'-whee.* She could see a *soup'-kss* emerge as she cried out her sorrow in the song she sang there by the water's edge.

(SOUP'-KSS enters and swims in front of KAI'-YAH while she sings. There may be a drum accompaniment.)

KAI'-YAH: *(Singing:)*
That is the game that you hunt
Emerging from the water, my child.
(repeat 2 times)

NARRATOR: *Kai'-yah* knew in her heart that her grandsons were lost, that someone had run off with them. She knew that a spell had been put on them!

(LIGHTS DOWN on KAI'-YAH. She and SOUP'-KSS exit. LIGHTS UP on village of the DWARVES. ALL unfreeze.)

NARRATOR: Now the Dwarves and the *Hot'-hot* raided and fought each other.

(MUSIC BEGINS: drums. HOT'-HOT enter with loud duck cries. They may swoop down from the tabletops. DWARVES battle with

them with great commotion. HOT'-HOT stab their feathers at the DWARVES and when one of the DWARVES gets hit, she holds the feather against her body, as if it is sticking in her like an arrow, and dies. Meanwhile, DA-HOOS-WHEE'-WHEE hide behind their canoe and watch the battle. DRUMS continue under the following.)

NARRATOR: These *Hot'-hot* killed the Dwarves with their feathers! The brothers thought that if they were to hit them with their paddles, they could have themselves a good duck feed.

(DA-HOOS-WHEE'-WHEE chase the HOT'-HOT with their paddles, hitting and killing some.)

HOT'-HOT SIAB: Raise your arms, my brothers! Those are human beings who are doing you in! Raise your arms, my brothers! Those are human beings who are doing you in!

(HOT'-HOT flap their wings, squawking loudly, and fly away in fright. MUSIC ENDS.)

NARRATOR: The brothers only hit them because they wanted food to eat. They looked at the dwarves. What had caused them to die? The brothers pulled a few of the feathers out.

(DA-HOOS-WHEE'-WHEE pull feathers out of a couple of dead DWARVES and they come back to life.)

NARRATOR: The Dwarves came back to life!

(DA-HOOS-WHEE'-WHEE continue to pull all the feathers out of the DWARVES and they all come back to life.)

NARRATOR: The brothers took the dead *Hot'-hot* off to one side. They cooked them and feasted a little.

(They do so. Meanwhile, DWARVES gather together.)

DWARF #3: These human beings have done us such a good deed, how can we return them to their home?

DWARF #4: They have given us life! Those *Hot'-hot* have been killing us for a long time.

DWARF #5: What can we do to get them back to their own homeland?

NARRATOR: The brothers were told that they would be taken home. The brothers went to the discarded dentalium shells that had been tossed into a huge pile by the dwarves after they had eaten the meat inside. They sorted out the biggest ones they could find.

(DA-HOOS-WHEE'-WHEE get some woven bags and fill them with shells – pantomime.)

NARRATOR: Dentalia are treasures here in our own time. Now *Da-hoos-whee'-whee* had lots of dentalia.

(DWARVES gather around DA-HOOS-WHEE'-WHEE.)

DWARF #6: We are going to return you folks. We shall call the *chuh-hoo-loo'*, the whale who travels all around. He will return you to your home.

DWARF #7: That *chuh-hoo-loo'* is an old person!

(DWARVES go to shore and call out.)

DWARVES: *Chuh-hoo-loo'! Chuh-hoo-loo'! (and so forth)*

(CHUH-HOO-LOO' enters.)

DWARF #8: *(to Chuh-hoo-loo')* We want you to return the two brothers, along with their *tkl'-ai.*

DWARF #9: You can just put them inside where you carry things and take them way over there. You know where they are from.

CHUH-HOO-LOO': *Aiii,* I know where these people are from. I pass by their homeland and I can hear an old woman mourning out loud. She must be their *kai'-yah.*

(DA-HOOS-WHEE'-WHEE load their bags of shells into their canoe and get in.)

CHUH-HOO-LOO': *(To Da-hoos-whee'-whee:)* I forbid a young female to look at me. If it is her moon-time, that is a serious taboo. The minute her eyes were to see me I would go into convulsions and thrash about!

(CHUH-HOO-LOO' takes the rope attached to the canoe and pulls them out to sea and they exit. LIGHTS DOWN. ALL exit. Change set: remove colorful longhouse facades and replace with plainer facades.)

SCENE 4

(Setting: The Lushootseed village, a few weeks later. LIGHTS UP. CHUH-HOO-LOO' & DA-HOOS-WHEE'-WHEE enter.)

NARRATOR: They traveled along until they could see a place where there were people living. Suddenly a young woman peeked at him.

(YOUNG WOMAN enters and looks at CHUH-HOO-LOO'. He immediately goes into convulsions, thrashing about, causing DA-HOOS-WHEE'-WHEE to be tossed about in their canoe. MUSIC: DRUMS. During the following narration the canoe gets tipped over and the bags of shells and DA-HOOS-WHEE'-WHEE fall out.)

NARRATOR: Bad! The minute she set eyes on him, the Chuh-hoo-loo' went into convulsions! Everything came spilling out. Somewhere on the other side of Seattle all of their dentalia spilled. They managed to get ashore and they went up on the beach.

(DA-HOOS-WHEE'-WHEE swim ashore and stand on one side of the stage and CHUH-HOO-LOO' exits. MUSIC ENDS.)

NARRATOR: They felt sad about their dentalia spilling out. Their spirit powers came to them as they felt sad about all the misfortune they had had to endure.

(SPIRIT POWERS enter – optional – and stand near DA-HOOS-WHEE'-WHEE.)

NARRATOR: They were seen by a child who was out playing.

(LITTLE BROTHER enters.)

LITTLE BROTHER: *Siab!*
DA-HOOS-WHEE'-WHEE: *Siab!* Are you our little brother?
LITTLE BROTHER: *Aiii!* We have been watching for you for a long time. Our people have suffered a lot of hardship and misery since you were lost.
OLDER BROTHER: You go home and tell the people that they are to gather everyone together. We will enter their home then. As soon as we come in we will sing our spirit songs.
LITTLE BROTHER: *Aiii!*

(LITTLE BROTHER goes over to village as some VILLAGERS &
STEPMOTHER enter there.)

LITTLE BROTHER: My brothers are over there. They told me to
come and tell you to gather everyone together, then they will come
here and come inside.

STEPMOTHER: You dirty little thing, do you have to say something
like that to us!

(She swats him. He runs back to DA-HOOS-WHEE'-WHEE.)

LITTLE BROTHER: My people just beat me! They think that I am
only talking.

YOUNGER BROTHER: You go ahead and tell them that we are their
children who have come. We will go there and go inside only after
they have followed our instructions, because we want to sing our
spirit songs now.

*(LITTLE BROTHER goes back to village and pantomimes talking
with BAHD.)*

NARRATOR: The bad woman who beat him is just his stepmother.
However, his father, *Bahd,* begins to believe his little son. He has
everyone put things in order to welcome those who have been lost.

*(ALL VILLAGERS enter and gather around village. DA-HOOS-
WHEE'-WHEE & SPIRIT POWERS come over to them during the
following narration.)*

NARRATOR: The brothers then come. Just as soon as they enter they
begin to sing their spirit songs.

(MUSIC BEGINS:)

DA-HOOS-WHEE'-WHEE & SPIRIT POWERS: *(Singing:)*
  We all fly like eagles
  Flying so high
  Circle 'round the universe
  With wings of pure light
  Hoo-wit-chee-chi-o
  Hoo-wee-i-o
  Hoo-wit-chee-chi-o
  Hoo-wee-i-o

(MUSIC ENDS.)

NARRATOR: Now things were changed. Deer and other food came down toward the shore.

(Optional – DEER enters.)

NARRATOR: Smelt came out of the water. All of the food came freely of its own accord. The bear came, and the *soup'-kss,* along with other food.

(Optional – SMELT, BEAR, SOUP'-KSS, and OTHER GAME enter.)

NARRATOR: That was what happened, and they all sang their spirit songs until everyone's power was strengthened.

(MUSIC BEGINS: drums, rattles, and so on.)

ALL: *(singing)*
    The earth is our mother
    We must take care of her
    The earth is our mother
    We must take care of her
    Hey-yung-a, ho-yung-a
    Hey-yung-yung
    Hey-yung-a, ho-yung-a
    Hey-yung-yung.
    Her sacred ground we walk upon
    With every step we take
    Her sacred ground we walk upon
    With every step we take
    Hey-yung-a, ho-yung-a
    Hey-yung-yung
    Hey-yung-a, ho-yung-a
    Hey-yung-yung.

    (MUSIC ENDS.)

NARRATOR: That is the end of the story concerning those who were lost.
ALL: *Hoi'-yah!* All is finished!

(LIGHTS DOWN.)

APPENDIX A: VOCABULARY LIST
OF FOREIGN LANGUAGE

LUSHOOTSEED	ENGLISH	PRONUNCIATION
aiii	yes	a'-eee
bahd	father	baad
chuh-hoo-loo'	whale	chuh-hoo-loo' (blow breath out, fast, on middle syllable)
da-hoos-whee'-whee	seal-hunting brothers, "the ones who hunt"	dah-hoos-whee'-whee (blow breath out on 2nd, 3rd and 4th syllables)
hoi'-yah	the end	hoy'-ah
hot'-hot	ducks	hot'-hot
huh-pai'	cedar	huh-pie'-ee
huy	good-bye	hoi
kai'-yah	grandmother	ki'-yah
siab	head man, or chief	see'-ahb
soup'-kss	seal	soup'-kss (catch in throat on "k")
tkl'-ai	canoe	kl-eye (make clicking sound in back of throat on "k")
tsah'-pah	grandfather	tsah'-pah
tsi siab / siab	hello (said to females / males)	tsee' see-ab / see'-ab
whee	no	whee (blow breath and pull in quickly at the end)

SETS LIST

LUSHOOTSEED VILLAGE:
   2-3 large, sturdy tables
   plain, dark cloths or 2-3 freestanding walls
   fire pit
   landscape backdrop (optional)

LAND OF THE DWARVES SHORE:
   large cedar log

VILLAGE OF THE DWARVES:
   same as for Lushootseed village, but with colorful house facades
   large pile of dentalium shells

HOW TO MAKE THE SETS

FREESTANDING WALLS (for longhouse facades)
   • very large, cardboard box
   • cardboard cutting knife
   • scissors
   • heavy butcher paper
   • tape or glue
   • markers, crayons or paint with brushes
   • colored paper or fabric (optional)

Cut box to create a freestanding wall with accordion folds. Cut butcher paper to size of the wall. Tape or glue paper to one side of the wall (if cardboard is plain white, you can eliminate this step). Draw picture of the longhouse on the wall with markers, crayons or paint. Colored paper or fabric can also be used to decorate the wall, using glue or tape. Lushootseed village longhouses are made of wood while on the reverse side of the wall, the longhouses of the Dwarves are very colorful and imaginative.

FIRE PIT
   • several cardboard paper towel tubes or other cardboard pieces, rolled like logs
   • flat piece of cardboard, approx. 30 cm. square
   • red, orange and/or yellow tissue paper
   • clear tape

Tape the tubes or other, log-shaped pieces of cardboard to the flat piece of cardboard. Tear the tissue paper into large pieces, stick them under and around the logs and tape with clear tape so that they jut up and out like flames.

LANDSCAPE BACKDROP

- heavy butcher paper
- markers, crayons or paint with brushes
- sturdy tape
- scissors

Cut butcher paper to fit across upstage wall. Draw scenes of the shores of Puget Sound with markers, crayons or paint. Make sure the artists understand which end is up and that drawings must be large enough to be seen from the audience. Tape to wall.

CEDAR LOG

- large piece of sturdy cardboard
- cutting tool
- strong tape
- brown paint & brushes or marker
- brown and green construction paper
- scissors
- glue

Cut cardboard to make large, long rectangle. Roll cardboard to make a tubular trunk and tape to secure. Use brown cardboard and add bark markings with markers, or paint the trunk. Branches, twigs, and leaves can be made out of cardboard and colored paper and taped or glued to trunk.

PILE OF DENTALIUM SHELLS

- large piece of cardboard
- sturdy tape
- white paint
- paintbrushes
- white paper
- scissors
- pencils
- glue

Roll the large piece of cardboard to make a cone shape and tape to secure. Paint the cone white. Cut white paper into squares approximately 10 cm square. Place a pencil on the corner of each square and tightly roll the paper around the pencil at a diagonal. These are the shells – they are larger than most real dentalium shells but for the purpose of props they should be large. With a single dab of glue on each shell, affix them to the cone base. There can be a few extra shells which are left to lie around loose on the floor, which the brothers put in their bags.

PROPS LIST

2 Canoes
2-3 Paddles
Fish (use plastic or cut out of paper)
Wooden Platters
Harpoon with Line
Rope (to tie canoe)
2 Soup Bowls
Net Bags
Duck Feathers

HOW TO MAKE THE PROPS

CANOES
Option #1:
- child's wagon
- 2 large pieces of sturdy cardboard
- cutting tool
- strong tape
- markers, crayons or paint with brushes
- butcher paper, scissors & glue (optional)

Draw and cut cardboard in the shape of the sides of a canoe. Decorate with markers, crayons or paint (Cover first with butcher paper, if needed.) Secure cardboard to both sides of the wagon with tape. Actors can sit in the wagon and propel it with their feet while steering with the handle turned inward.

Option #2:
- very large, cardboard box
- strong tape
- paint
- paint brushes
OR:
- butcher paper
- scissors
- glue
- markers or crayons

Fold and tape open both the top and bottom of the box. Either paint the outside of the box or cover it with butcher paper and decorate with markers or crayons. Actors propel the boat by walking inside it while holding up the sides with their hands.

PADDLES
- 1 or 2 long poles, such as from a broom or mop
- 1 or 2 pieces of thick cardboard
- cardboard cutting tool
- tape
- paint, as needed

Draw a large circle, slightly oblong, on the cardboard, approximately 30 cm long. Use thick cardboard so it will not get easily bent. Draw a small column attached to the bottom of the circle, a few cm wide and long (for attaching to the pole), and cut out. Place the cardboard round near the top of the pole and wrap tape around the column, securing it to the pole. Paint as needed.

HARPOON
- long, cardboard tube (such as for wrapping paper)
- small piece of thick cardboard
- cardboard cutting tool
- string or thin rope
- sturdy tape

Draw spear point on thick cardboard, including a small column at the bottom for taping to the tube, and cut out. Secure to the end of the tube with tape. Cut a length of string or rope several meters long. Tie one end of the string to the tube at the end opposite the end with the spear point and tape to secure. Older Brother will throw the harpoon while holding onto the other end of the string. Seal will catch the harpoon and hold it as if it has been speared while Older Brother continues to hold on to the end of the string.

DUCK FEATHERS
- colored construction paper
- scissors
- plastic straws
- clear tape

Draw large feather shapes on paper and cut out. Feather the edges by making little clips with the scissors. Cut plastic straws to length slightly longer than the feathers. Place each straw down the center of each feather, with the extra length of straw serving as the stem. Tape to secure. Actors can hold feathers by the stems. Real feathers can be used instead.

APPENDIX D: COSTUMES

DA-HOOS-WHEE'-WHEE & ALL VILLAGERS: traditional Lushootseed costumes, or plain pants & shirts
SOUP'-KSS: plain gray or black leotard & tights or pants & shirt
DWARVES: colorful pants & shirts

DUCKS: plain colored pants & shirts with plastic duckbills or duckbill base-
ball-type hats and wings made of cloth pinned to shirt sleeves
CHUH-HOO-LOO': plain gray or black leotard & tights or pants & shirt
SPIRIT POWERS: fanciful costumes, perhaps with gauze fabric capes and
headpieces.
BEAR, DEER, SMELT & OTHER GAME: plain colored pants & shirts or
leotard and tights, with ears, tails, and so forth, added.

APPENDIX E: SOUND & MUSIC

MUSIC:
When *Da-hoos-whee'-whee* chase phantom *soup'-kss:* drums and rattles
During Dwarves & *Hot'-hot* battle: drums and rattles
Song: "We All Fly Like Eagles" – included
Song: "The Earth Is Our Mother" – included
Song: "Wearing our Long-Wing Feathers" (included, see Appendix E for
Legend of the Seasons)
Other songs (optional)

APPENDIX F: LUSHOOTSEED SALISH CULTURE
Sources: *Haboo, Native American Stories of Puget Sound* by Vi Hilbert
(University of Washington Press) and The Eye of the Changer by Muriel Ringstad
(Alaska Northwest Publishing Company)

LITERATURE
In the past, all of the culture of these peoples had to be committed to
memory; thus, their historians developed excellent memories in order to pass
on important information to later generations. When the culture was solely
oral, as some elders would prefer to have it remain, the legends and other
information were recited often in order to keep them alive and point out
moral lessons. We do not know how long it has taken for these stories to come
down to us, for they did not use the kind of calendar we use today. The
Lushootseed peoples marked time by referring to especially remarkable occa-
sions, such as the year of the solar eclipse or the time before the British people
came. Today, the art of storytelling among the Lushootseed-speaking peoples
is nearly forgotten as television and books have supplanted the roles of the
Lushootseed raconteurs.
All of their legends are like gems with many facets. They need to be read,
savored, and reread from many angles. Listeners are expected to listen carefully
and learn why a story is being told. They are not told directly the meaning of
the stories but are instead allowed the dignity of finding their own personal
interpretation. All of the stories in Lushootseed culture are rich in humor,

much of which pokes fun at pretentiousness. They can laugh at themselves and others in a way that is not malicious and which is mutually enjoyable and frequently uplifting.

LANGUAGE

Lushootseed is one of some twenty Native languages comprising the Salish family, spoken over much of Washington, British Columbia, and parts of Idaho, Montana, and Oregon. Lushootseed itself is the name of the Native language of the Puget Sound region, of which there are many dialects.

Translating the literature of one language into another is never easy, especially when the cultures involved are extremely dissimilar and when the translator must render in writing what has been an oral tradition. Subtleties of the Lushootseed language and oral delivery, such as tone of voice, vocal mannerisms, rhythm, pitch, and the effects of syntax and repetitions, cannot be fully expressed in written English. For example, there is no Lushootseed word for love, so it's meaning and nuances must be recognized from the signals expressed in the oral delivery.

In Lushootseed culture, everything is possible because they have no word for "can't." They also have no words that say "hello," "good morning," "good night,"or "thank you." All these meanings are expressed through phrases or by physical gestures. For example, thankfulness is expressed by a phrase that translates as "You have done me a great favor/I appreciate what you have done for me" or by raising both arms and slightly moving the open palms up and down.

SPIRITUAL VALUES

All of the Lushootseed stories give expression to the most important values of the culture. These values, as remembered and translated by Vi Hilbert, are listed below. Many of the Lushootseed values are phrased in the negative but are here expressed in the positive:

Respect (Hold Sacred) all of the Earth
Respect (Hold Sacred) All of the Spirits
Remember (Hold Sacred) the Creator
Be Honest (Don't You Dare Lie!)
Be Generous (Be Helpful to Your People In Any Way You Can!)
Be Compassionate (Feel Forgiveness For Others!)
Be Clean (You Will Be Washed/Keep Washing Away All Badness [Dirt and Sin-Crime])
Be Industrious (And You Will Work Always, Don't Be Lazy!)

Today, many Lushootseed people are preserving and activating the spiritual beliefs of their ancestors. In the past, Lushootseed people believed they needed a spirit power to help them with special tasks. At around age four, boys went away by themselves to fast and wait for their spirit powers to make themselves known to the boys. Women also had spirit helpers for their special tasks. Animals, fish, and everything in nature each possessed a spirit, just as humans do. Ceremonies were created to show good intentions to the spirits. For example, the bones of the salmon were thrown back in the water in order to thank the salmon spirits and so that new salmon would be generated from them.

SOCIAL VALUES

Lushootseed peoples are told again and again not to disgrace themselves or their people under any circumstances. Still, they appreciate anyone smart enough to get something done by fooling someone else. Their stories are often about people with animal names so that the humor of human foibles and frailties can be more openly laughed about.

In public, however, Native people take care to not make anyone feel embarrassed or unwanted, and they genuinely appreciate differences between people. Although the characters in their stories often get themselves in lots of trouble, they are not wiped out at the end. Instead, they are allowed to stew in their own folly and figure their own way out of the situation. Disapproval of bad habits or behavior is shown by temporarily ignoring someone or by ridiculing them, but this is meant as a way to help the person overcome their problem. It is believed that ultimately, everyone should be made to feel welcome and important.

HOUSING

In the past, the Lushootseed lived in villages of four or five cedar plank houses, called longhouses. Each longhouse sheltered several related families and as many as forty people lived in each one. The longhouses measured approximately one hundred feet long and forty feet wide. They were dark and smoky inside, as the doorway was small and there were no windows. A plank in the roof was lifted up to let out smoke from the cooking fires. Fires were kept burning on the dirt floor in front of each family's quarters. From the ceiling hung chunks of smoked salmon, strings of smoked clams, and dried roots and herbs.

Along the inside walls were built two wide platforms, one above the other. The people slept on the upper platform and worked on the lower one, which was wider. The space underneath the lower platform was used for storage. The women sewed cattail leaves together for mats, which were hung between each family's section for privacy and warmth. Mattresses and sitting pads were also made of woven cattails.

CLOTHING

Their clothing was made of cedar bark which had been shredded and pounded. Robes and blankets were made of shredded cedar bark mixed with fireweed fluff and feathers or dog or goat wool, or were made of bird or animal skins or furs sewn together. Ponchos were made of cattail leaves and hats were made of tightly twined cedar bark.

UTENSILS & TOOLS

Kitchen utensils were carved out of wood by the men. The women made mats and baskets of grasses, roots, twigs, and other materials gathered during the summer. These materials were soaked and split, cured and sometimes dyed. They had no metal. Tools were made of horn, bone, or stone, with wooden handles. To cook, women heated stones in a fire and then, using greenwood tongs, placed the stones into tightly coiled cedar root baskets. When the stones cooled, they were replaced with hot ones from the fire.

CANOES

Their way of life was based on canoes. Canoes were made of dugout cedar logs and their size and shape depended on their use. Sharp-ended canoes with high prows were for rough water, as the prows could cut through the water like a wedge and blunt-ended canoes were for use on rivers and still waters. The canoes were thirty to fifty feet long and could carry twenty to thirty people and their luggage. Extra curved projections at the bow and stern were carved from separate pieces of cedar and attached to the canoes with pegs and withes of thin cedar limbs. Canoes in use were kept floating in the cove in front of the village. Those not in use were turned over on the beach above the tide line and covered with mats to protect them from the sun.

THE EARTH IS OUR MOTHER

Moderato

traditional Native American

The earth is our mo - ther, we must take
sa - cred ground we step u - pon with ev - ery

care of her, the earth is our mo - ther, we must take
step we take, her sa-cred ground we step u - pon with ev - ery

care of her. Hey yung- a, ho yung- a,
step we take.

hey yung, yung. Hey yung- a, ho yung- a,

1.
hey yung, yung. Her

2.
yung.

WE ALL FLY LIKE EAGLES

Moderato

We all fly like ea - gles (we all fly like ea - gles)

Fly - ing so high (fly - ing so high)

Cir - cle 'round the un - i -verse (cir - cle 'round the un - i -verse) With

wings of pure light (with wings of pure light)

Hoo - wit -chee - chi - o (hoo - wit -chee - chi - o)

Hoo-wee- i - o (hoo-wee- i - - o) Hoo - wit -chee

chi - o (hoo - wit -chee - chi - o) Hoo - wee - i -

o (hoo - wee - i - o)

EAST OF THE SUN AND WEST OF THE MOON
(Norway)

This story has been circulating and changing for many generations and you'll surely recognize it's famous cousin, *Beauty and the Beast*. I much prefer this story to *Beauty and the Beast*, especially the Disney movie version, because here the heroine is much more proactive in seeking her fulfillment, her mother and her mother's wisdom are preserved as a key element to Beauty's process of discovery, and because the Prince is so much more attractive as a White Bear—a beautiful symbol of wild nature—than an ugly beast. Here I've continued in the tradition of adapting and retelling the story by placing it in a science fiction genre. The basic story is still the same, but modern kids may relate to its outer space setting, which also allows for some creative production designs.

This epic production is suitable for a large cast and can be produced in collaboration with many classes or groups. There are lots of characters and lines, wonderful possibilities for music and dance, and great creative potential for designing and building sets, costumes and props, including spaceships. A separate sound effects and music ensemble can be employed and music can be either selected from tapes and CD's or played live. The movement of the Four Winds can be choreographed and performed by a special group of dancers, and a song and/or dance can be added to the very end.

This play can be integrated with a unit on the four directions: east, west, south, and north. The directions have many correspondences in Native American, as well as other earth-based, religions. The music and colors selected for each can reflect the qualities represented by each direction.

RUNNING TIME OF SHOW *(approximate):*

30-35 minutes

REHEARSAL TIME NEEDED:

18-20 hours (more for large cast)

OTHER PRODUCTION TIME NEEDED:

10-12 hours

CAST SIZE:

Minimum: 7, plus Narrator (except for the actors playing Beauty and Bear/Prince, all other actors can play more than one role. Servant and Children lines can be consolidated.)

Maximum: 50-60 (There can be numerous Children and Servants)

Multiple Class/Group show:

Group #1 = leads: Beauty, Bear/Prince, Mother, Father, Queen, and Princess; plus Servants and Children

Group #2 = Old Women/Men, Aliens, and their spaceships. This group invents, builds, and operates the spaceships, as well as possibly other props and sets.

Group #3 = Winds (dance and movement)

Group #4 = Wedding Song and/or Dance at the end of the show

GENDER OF CHARACTERS:

Children, Old Women/Men, Winds, Servants, and Aliens can be played as either female or male; all other characters should be played as designated.

CHARACTERS:

NARRATOR	THIRD OLD WOMAN / MAN
MOTHER	SPACE HORSES (optional)
FATHER	EAST WIND
BEAUTY – their youngest daughter	WEST WIND
	SOUTH WIND
CHILDREN – Beauty's sisters and brothers	NORTH WIND
	PRINCESS LONGNOSE
WHITE BEAR / PRINCE	QUEEN – mother of the Princess
FIRST OLD WOMAN / MAN	SERVANTS – of the Queen
SECOND OLD WOMAN/ MAN	ALIENS

SCENE 1

(Setting: On one side of the stage is the house of MOTHER &
FATHER and their CHILDREN and on the other side is the castle of
the BEAR. The house is very poor, bare, and crowded. Upstage, there is
a freestanding, interior wall. There is a door which leads into the house
– it could be part of this wall, a curtain, or an existing door in your
building. The BEAR'S castle consists of a large, beautiful bed, possibly
with a canopy, and one chair. There may also be an interior wall. The
castle is very grand and decorated in gold and silver. For now, the bed
and chair are hidden by a freestanding wall, decorated as a castle wall,
or by a curtain. LIGHTS UP.)

NARRATOR: There once lived a very poor couple who lived with
their children on a cold and snowy planet. The couple had at one
time been very prosperous merchants of the Seventh Galaxy, but
had lost their fortune when their entire fleet of spaceships were
destroyed in the fiery explosion of a star gone supernova.

(MOTHER, FATHER, BEAUTY & CHILDREN enter. They all
wear poor clothing.)

CHILD #1: It's cold in here!
CHILD #2: I'm hungry!

(ALL CHILDREN whine and complain to MOTHER & FATHER
who try to pacify them. BEAUTY, however, stands to one side, uncom-
plaining. SOUND: door knocking. FATHER opens the door and there
stands BEAR. The children scream and hide with fright.)

BEAR: Good evening.
FATHER: *(Nervous.)* Good evening!
BEAR: Sir, if you will give me your youngest daughter, I will make you
as rich as you are now poor.
FATHER: *(Thinks.)* Hmm...I must speak with my daughter first. Wait
here.

(BEAR comes inside, closes the door, and politely waits. Meanwhile,
FATHER goes over to BEAUTY.)

FATHER: Uh, Beauty, dear, there's a white bear here who has promised
to make us all rich if only you'll go with him!

BEAUTY: No.

FATHER: But Beauty, just look at how hungry your sisters and brothers are! And your poor mother is shivering with cold! Will you deny them the chance for a little comfort?

BEAUTY: I will not agree to go with the white bear.

(FATHER goes back over to BEAR.)

FATHER: I'll need a little more time to persuade her. Come again next Thursday evening for an answer.

BEAR: All right.

(BEAR exits. ALL gather around BEAUTY and whine and complain, – ad lib – trying to persuade her to go with him so that they can be rich. BEAUTY refuses to budge. LIGHTS DOWN. LIGHTS UP. BEAUTY is finishing packing a small backpack. MOTHER is crying softly.)

FATHER: You're a real sport to go with him, Beauty! Thanks for changing your mind!

BEAUTY: I couldn't take the guilt any longer!

(SOUND: Door knocking. BEAUTY hugs her family good-bye, goes to the door and opens it. There stands BEAR.)

BEAUTY: All right, let's go.

BEAR: Are you afraid?

BEAUTY: No. Should I be?

BEAR: Hold tight to my coat and there's no danger.

(BEAUTY "climbs on his back" by placing hands on his shoulders from behind, holding tight to his fur. They exit. LIGHTS DOWN. ALL exit. NOTE: Selected MUSIC can be played during some or all scene changes throughout the play.)

SCENE 2

(Setting: Castle of the BEAR, a few hours later. LIGHTS UP. BEAR & BEAUTY enter, she riding on his back. They stop and she gets off.)

BEAR: This is my castle. Here you shall have everything you desire!

BEAUTY: Right now, all I want to do is go to sleep!

BEAR: All you have to do is ring this silver bell and all your wishes shall be granted.

(BEAR gives her bell and exits. BEAUTY rings bell. MUSIC BEGINS: Bear's Theme – some soft, lovely music plays as the free-standing wall or curtain in front of the bed is removed. If using a free-standing wall, it could now be placed behind the bed to act as an interior wall. MUSIC continues as BEAUTY gets into bed and falls asleep. SOME LIGHTS DOWN. BEAR/PRINCE enters, without his bear costume. He sits in chair and watches BEAUTY for a few moments, then falls asleep, snoring softly. BEAUTY wakes up at the sound, sits up and looks at him with curiosity but cannot see him well in the semidarkness. She lays down again.

ALL LIGHTS DOWN. BEAR exits. MUSIC ENDS. LIGHTS UP. BEAUTY wakes up and looks at the empty chair.)

BEAUTY: Hmm...

(She rings the silver bell. SOUND: Chimes or soft bells. A beautiful dress magically appears – it can be lowered from the ceiling on a string, appear over the top of an interior wall, carried in by fairies, or appear by some other device. BEAUTY takes dress and exits. LIGHTS DOWN.)

NARRATOR: For awhile Beauty was happy, for she had everything she wanted when she rang the silver bell. Every night after she had put out the light, the strange man came into her bedroom and slept in the chair, and every morning before dawn he was gone again.
After a time, Beauty began to miss her family. The White Bear agreed to take her to visit them.

(BEAR & BEAUTY enter. She now wears the beautiful dress.)

BEAR: And remember what I told you: *Never speak alone with your mother* or you will bring misfortune to both of us!
BEAUTY: I promise!

(She "climbs on his back" as before, holding tight to his coat. They exit. LIGHTS DOWN. Change set: Turn around the interior wall of MOTHER & FATHER'S house and may add fancy pillows, furniture, and so on.)

SCENE 3

(Setting: The house of MOTHER & FATHER. They are now fabulously wealthy: the interior wall is turned around to show the wealthy side and fancy pillows and furniture may be added. MOTHER, FATHER & CHILDREN enter. They are all wearing rich clothes. LIGHTS UP. SOUND: door knocking. FATHER opens the door and there stands BEAUTY, while BEAR waits for her just outside the door.)

ALL: Beauty! You're home! *(and so forth)*

(ALL rush over and hug her, all talking at once, showing her their new clothes and talking about how rich they are – ad lib.)

MOTHER: Children! Give Beauty some peace!

(ALL quiet down.)

MOTHER: Come with me, Beauty, for I want to speak with you alone.
BEAUTY: *(Worried.)* Uh...not now, Mother...
MOTHER: Please, Beauty, I want to speak with you alone!
BEAUTY: No, I must not!
MOTHER: What?
BEAUTY: Uh...I mean...we can talk later!
MOTHER: Beauty, I insist! I want to speak with you *alone!*

(MOTHER pulls BEAUTY aside.)

MOTHER: Now, tell me everything!
BEAUTY: Mother, there's a man who comes into my room every night, but I never see him because it's too dark and he's always gone before dawn! I want to see him, for during the day I'm so lonely!
MOTHER: Dear me! It may be a troll! But here, take this candle so that you can see him at night.

(She gives BEAUTY a candle which she puts in her pocket.)

MOTHER: And take care to not drop any candle wax on him!

(SOUND: Door knocking.)

BEAUTY: That's the White Bear! I must leave!

(She says good-bye to ALL and they hug her and say good-bye. Mean-

while, FATHER opens the door and BEAR is standing there. BEAU-TY exits with him. LIGHTS DOWN. ALL exit.)

SCENE 4

(Setting: The BEAR'S castle, a few hours later. LIGHTS UP. BEAR & BEAUTY enter, she riding on his back. They stop and she gets off.)

BEAR: Did you speak alone with your mother?

BEAUTY: Uh...yes.

BEAR: *(Upset.)* If you listened to your mother's advice, you will bring misfortune to both of us!

BEAUTY: I won't, I promise! I'm going to bed now – goodnight!

(He exits as she rings her silver bell. MUSIC BEGINS: Bear's Theme, which plays under the following. BEAUTY gets into bed and pretends to sleep.

SOME LIGHTS DOWN. BEAR/PRINCE enters, without bear costume, sits in the chair and falls asleep, snoring softly.

BEAUTY sits up and gets out the candle and lights it – or use battery-operated electric candle. She leans over him, trying to get a closer look, and in so doing "drips" candle wax on him. He wakes up with a start; MUSIC ENDS and LIGHTS UP.)

BEAR/PRINCE: AAAHHH!!! What have you done! If you had only waited for one year I should have been saved!

BEAUTY: What are you talking about?!!

BEAR/PRINCE: A wicked queen has cast a spell on me, so that I'm a bear by day and a man by night! But now I must leave you and go back to her! She lives in a castle on the Blue Planet which lies east of the sun and west of the moon. In the same castle lives a princess with a nose two meters long, and now I must marry her!

BEAUTY: Oh, can't I go with you?!!

(SOUND BEGINS: Wind Storm. BEAR/PRINCE is magically swept up by the wind and is being carried away. They have to yell over the noise of the wind storm.)

BEAR/PRINCE: Impossible! AAAHHH!!!

(He is being carried away, despite his efforts to resist. BEAUTY tries to follow but cannot.)

BEAUTY: I will try to find you!!

(BEAR exits. SOUND ENDS. BEAUTY stands all alone, bewildered. She exits. LIGHTS DOWN. Change set: Remove MOTHER & FATHER'S HOUSE and BEAR'S CASTLE; set up any sets needed for outer space/OLD WOMEN/THE WINDS.)

SCENE 5

(Setting: Outer space and the planets of the OLD WOMEN, sometime later. There need be no sets but simply various locations around the stage or performance space where BEAUTY encounters the OLD WOMEN and their spaceships. There could be an outer space backdrop on the wall. The spaceships are fanciful creations of the cast and can be made of large boxes which are open underneath so that the actor simply walks inside it, holding up the sides of the box with her hands; small, decorated wagons which are propelled by the feet or by a rope pulled from backstage; or other devices, including the use of other actors who operate the ships. Spaceships can also be replaced with "Space Horses," played by other actors.

LIGHTS UP. BEAUTY enters. She is wearing her poor clothes and carries her backpack. FIRST OLD WOMAN enters in her spaceship and approaches BEAUTY. There may be SOUND EFFECTS or MUSIC for each spaceship, such as played by percussion instruments or noisemakers.)

BEAUTY: Excuse me, do you know the way to the Blue Planet that lies east of the sun and west of the moon?

FIRST OLD WOMAN: You must be looking for the Prince! I don't know how to get there, but I'll lend you my spaceship and you can ride to my neighbor – perhaps she can tell you!

(She gets out of her spaceship and BEAUTY gets in.)

FIRST OLD WOMAN: When you get there, just push this button and my spaceship will return to me. *(Indicates button on ship.)*
Oh, and you better take this golden apple with you. You might find a use for it!

(She gives BEAUTY apple.)

BEAUTY: Thanks and good-bye!
FIRST OLD WOMAN: Good-bye!

*(BEAUTY travels around as FIRST OLD WOMAN exits and SEC-
OND OLD WOMAN enters – possible SOUND EFFECTS or
MUSIC of spaceships. SECOND OLD WOMAN is either driving her
spaceship or it's parked nearby. BEAUTY stops and gets out of her
spaceship. She pushes the button and the spaceship exits. She goes up to
SECOND OLD WOMAN.)*

SECOND OLD WOMAN: You must be the girl looking for the
Prince! I don't know the way to the Blue planet either, but you can
borrow my spaceship and ride to my neighbor – perhaps she can
tell you!

(She gets out of her spaceship and BEAUTY gets in.)

SECOND OLD WOMAN: When you get there, just pull this lever
and my spaceship will return to me. *(Indicates lever.)* Oh, and you
better take this golden carding-comb with you. You might find a
use for it!

(She gives BEAUTY the carding-comb.)

BEAUTY: Thanks and good-bye!
SECOND OLD WOMAN: Good-bye!

*(BEAUTY travels around as SECOND OLD WOMAN exits and
THIRD OLD WOMAN enters another area of the stage. Possible
SOUND EFFECTS or MUSIC of spaceships. THIRD OLD
WOMAN is either driving her spaceship, or it's parked nearby. BEAU-
TY comes up to her, stops, and gets out of her spaceship. She pulls the
lever and the spaceship exits.)*

THIRD OLD WOMAN: What took you so long?!! Well, I, too, don't
know the way to the Blue Planet but you can borrow my spaceship
and ride to the East Wind and ask him – perhaps he can blow you
there!

(She gets out of her spaceship and BEAUTY gets in.)

THIRD OLD WOMAN: When you get there, just turn this dial and my spaceship will return to me. *(Indicates dial.)* Oh, and you better take this golden spinning wheel with you. You might find a use for it!

(She gives BEAUTY the spinning wheel.)

BEAUTY: Thanks and good-bye!
THIRD OLD WOMAN: Good-bye!

(BEAUTY exits in spaceship and THIRD OLD WOMAN exits. Possible SOUND EFFECTS or MUSIC of spaceship. LIGHTS DOWN.)

SCENE 6

(Setting: Outer space, continuation of the last scene. For the following scenes with the WINDS, there need be no sets but there should be interesting places for their movements, such as on tabletops, or through the audience, and so forth. The WINDS each have a distinctive movement or dance which matches their theme music. When they travel with BEAUTY they "blow" her. Each WIND can be represented by one or more actors. For each WIND, the lines can be spoken by one actor, divided up among a few actors, or spoken in unison by a small group. If the WINDS are played by small groups, the lines can be changed to read: "We are...", and so on. MUSIC BEGINS: East Wind Theme. LIGHTS UP. EAST WIND enters, moving to music. BEAUTY enters in spaceship. She stops, gets out, turns dial and spaceship exits. MUSIC DOWN under the following.)

EAST WIND:
I am the East Wind!
Eagle of Dawn!
But I know not the way
To which you are drawn.
Come, ride the whirlwind
That I love the best
And I shall take you to
the Wind from the West!

(MUSIC UP: BEAUTY moves with EAST WIND as they travel around the performance space. MUSIC CHANGES: West Wind Theme, as WEST WIND enters another area, moving to music.

BEAUTY & EAST WIND move over to WEST WIND. MUSIC DOWN under the following.)

WEST WIND:
  I am the West Wind!
  Serpent of Water!
  But I know not the way
  For the merchants' young daughter.
  Come, ride the rainstorm
  That pours from my mouth
  And I shall take you to
  The Wind from the South!

  (MUSIC UP: BEAUTY moves with WEST WIND as they travel around the performance space and EAST WIND exits. MUSIC CHANGES: South Wind Theme, as SOUTH WIND enters another area, moving to music. BEAUTY & WEST WIND move over to SOUND WIND. MUSIC DOWN under the following.)

SOUTH WIND:
  I am the South Wind!
  Lion of the Sun!
  But I know not the way,
  To your Prince, fairest one.
  Come, ride my flames
  And we shall go forth
  To the strongest of us all,
  The Wind from the North!

  (MUSIC UP: BEAUTY moves with SOUTH WIND as they travel around the performance space and WEST WIND exits. MUSIC CHANGES: North Wind Theme, as NORTH WIND enters another area, moving to music. BEAUTY & SOUTH WIND move over to NORTH WIND. MUSIC DOWN under the following.)

NORTH WIND: *(Very loudly.)* WHAT DO YOU WANT?!!!

  (MUSIC STOPS.)

SOUTH WIND: Oh, you needn't be so harsh! It's I, your own sister, and I have with me the girl who is looking for the Prince who lives on the Blue Planet that lies east of the sun and west of the moon. Do you know how to get there?

NORTH WIND: YES, I DO KNOW THE WAY! IT'S A LONG WAY AND WILL TAKE ALL MY MIGHT, BUT IF YOU ARE NOT AFRAID I WILL TRY TO BLOW YOU THERE!

BEAUTY: I'm not afraid!

(MUSIC UP: BEAUTY moves with NORTH WIND and they and SOUTH WIND exit. LIGHTS DOWN; MUSIC continues during scene change. Change set: Set up the castle of the QUEEN.)

SCENE 7

(Setting: Castle of the QUEEN, a few light-years later. On one side of the stage is an exterior wall with a window in it – can use the same wall as for the BEAR'S castle, or use an already existing window in your building. Near the wall, or as part of the wall, is an entrance way to the castle, which can be pantomimed. There is an open area center stage which represents the castle interior and there may be an interior wall here. Nearby is the bedroom of the PRINCE, with a bed and chair, and possibly an interior wall. LIGHTS UP. BEAUTY & NORTH WIND enter, totally exhausted, and stop just outside the exterior wall of the castle. MUSIC ENDS.)

NORTH WIND: *(Gasping.)* Phew! Well, here we are on the Blue Planet! And this is the castle of the Queen who has imprisoned your Prince until her marries Princess Longnose.
Are you afraid?

BEAUTY: Not a bit! Thanks for the ride!

NORTH WIND: I'm going to have to rest for a few days...Good luck!

(NORTH WIND exits.)

QUEEN: *(Offstage, screeching.)* SERVANTS!! SERVANTS!!

(BEAUTY quickly finds a hiding place somewhere, as QUEEN enters.)

QUEEN: Where are you miserable servants when I need you?!!

(SERVANTS #1 & #2 enter, quaking with fear.)

SERVANTS: Yes, your majesty?

QUEEN: I didn't go to all the trouble of imprisoning you here on this planet so that I could wait all morning for you to do my bidding! Princess Longnose is waiting in her room.

(She points up to the window in the wall.)

QUEEN: She must be fitted for her bridal gown right away, for her wedding to the Prince is to take place in only three days!

SERVANT #1: But...but, your majesty...Whenever the royal dressmaker tries to fit a gown on Princess Longnose, the Princess's nose rips the fabric!

QUEEN: Then OFF with her HEAD!!!

SERVANT #2: Oh, your majesty, no need to cut off the Princess's whole head in order to solve the nose problem!

QUEEN: IDIOT!!! Off with the *dressmaker's* head, not the Princess's!!! And your own as well, if you don't get busy right now!!!

(QUEEN chases SERVANTS offstage. BEAUTY comes out of her hiding place and sits beneath the castle wall. She gets out the golden apple and begins to play with it. PRINCESS LONGNOSE opens the window and looks out. Her nose is absurdly long. She sees BEAUTY and watches her, entranced.)

PRINCESS LONGNOSE: *(Calling out.)* Girl! Girl!

(BEAUTY looks up at her.)

PRINCESS LONGNOSE: What do you want for that golden apple?

BEAUTY: It's not for sale, neither for gold nor money.

PRINCESS LONGNOSE: Well, what do you want for it then? I'll give you what you ask!

BEAUTY: You can have it if tonight I may sit by the bedside of the Prince who lives here.

PRINCESS LONGNOSE: Well...all right. Now give it to me!

(BEAUTY gives her the apple.)

PRINCESS LONGNOSE: Come back tonight!

(PRINCESS closes the window and BEAUTY exits. LIGHTS DOWN.)

SCENE 8

(Setting: Same, that evening. LIGHTS UP. PRINCE enters his room.)

PRINCESS: *(Offstage.)* Oh, Princey!! Princey Poo!!

(PRINCE makes a sour face. PRINCESS enters, carrying a goblet.)

PRINCESS: There's my silly teddy bear! Before you go to bed, drink some of this yummy berry juice I brought for you!

PRINCE: Well, I do love berries...

(He takes the goblet and drinks all the juice – pantomime – while she stares at him with a silly, lovesick look on her face. He gives her back the goblet.)

PRINCE: Goodnight.

(He gets into bed. She still stands there, staring at him.)

PRINCE: *(Glaring.)* I *said*, GOODNIGHT!!

(She doesn't move, still smiling stupidly.)

PRINCE: Can't you hear?!! I *said*, G......

(He instantly conks out, fast asleep, snoring softly. PRINCESS giggles and leaves his room. Just outside his room, SERVANT #3 enters.)

PRINCESS: Servant, there's a girl who'll be coming to the castle this evening. I told her she could sit in the Prince's room tonight and watch him sleep because I feel sorry for her! She's hopelessly ugly and it's sure she'll never attract anyone as good looking as MY Prince!

(PRINCESS giggles and exits. BEAUTY enters at castle entrance and rings the bell. SOUND: Bell. SERVANT #3 goes to the entrance and opens it.)

SERVANT #3: *(Astounded.)* Are *you* the girl who is to sit in the Prince's room tonight?!!

BEAUTY: Yes, I am.

SERVANT #3: But she said you were...Oh, well, follow me.

(SERVANT #3 leads her to the PRINCE'S room and exits.)

BEAUTY: Oh, my White Bear Prince! I've found you at last!

(He still sleeps. She shakes him.)

BEAUTY: Wake up! It's me, Beauty!

(She keeps shaking him, to no avail.)

BEAUTY: Oh, why won't you wake up?!! (and so on.)

(She keeps trying to wake him, but finally gives up and sits in the chair, crying. LIGHTS DOWN. LIGHTS UP, the next morning. BEAUTY is asleep in the chair. PRINCESS enters and roughly shakes BEAUTY awake.)

PRINCESS: You've had your look at the Prince, now get out of here!

(BEAUTY sadly exits. LIGHTS DOWN. PRINCE & PRINCESS exit.)

SCENE 9

(Setting, the same, two nights later. LIGHTS UP. SERVANTS #4, #5, #6 & #7 enter.)

SERVANT #4: Have you seen that beautiful girl who's been coming to the castle the last three days?

SERVANT #5: Yesterday she traded the Princess a golden carding-comb for the chance to sit in the Prince's room, but he never woke up!

SERVANT #6: Why won't he wake up? Something crazy's going on here!

SERVANT #7: Let's go tell him!

(They go to PRINCE'S room as he enters there.)

SERVANT #4: Excuse us, your majesty, but there's something we think you should know.

SERVANT #5: There's a very beautiful girl who's been coming to your room to see you the last two nights!

PRINCE: What!! Why haven't I been told?!!

SERVANT #6: Well, sir, you've been as sound asleep as a bear in hibernation and she hasn't been able to wake you!

SERVANT #7: *(Looking out the door.)* She's coming!

(ALL SERVANTS hurriedly exit. PRINCESS enters, with goblet.)

PRINCESS: Time for your beddie-bye drinkie-poo, my silly teddy bear!

(She gives him the goblet.)

PRINCE: Say, your nose is dripping!
PRINCESS: Oh, dear!

(She turns away from him for a moment, pulls out her handkerchief and blows her nose loudly. Meanwhile, he tosses out the contents of the goblet – pantomime. She turns back to him and he hands her the goblet.)

PRINCE: Goodnight!

(He gets into bed and immediately begins snoring. PRINCESS stares at him for a moment, giggles, and exits. BEAUTY enters at castle entrance and rings bell. SOUND: bell. SERVANT #3 goes to entrance, leads BEAUTY to PRINCE'S room, then exits. PRINCE suddenly jumps up.)

PRINCE: Beauty!!!
BEAUTY: You're awake!!!

(They hug.)

PRINCE: You're just in time, for I'm to be married to Princess Snot-nose tomorrow! But I have a plan...

(They whisper together as LIGHTS DOWN. They exit.)

SCENE 10

(Setting: The same, the next day. The washtub and shirts props are back-stage. MUSIC BEGINS: Princess's Wedding Music. LIGHTS UP. ALL SERVANTS enter. They may have wedding decorations, such as streamers or balloons, which they put up around the set. PRINCE enters and stands center and BEAUTY enters and stands quietly off to one side. QUEEN & PRINCESS make a grand entrance. PRINCESS wears a wedding gown and a bridal veil that drapes across her nose. QUEEN stands center, between PRINCE & PRINCESS. MUSIC ENDS.)

QUEEN: Let the royal wedding begin!
PRINCE: Wait! Before I can marry, I must first see what my bride can do!

(He holds up a white shirt that has three big stains on it.)

PRINCE: My wedding shirt has three candle wax stains on it. I will not marry any woman except the one who is able to wash out these stains!

SERVANT #8: *(An aside to Servant #9.)* Why doesn't he do his own laundry?!

SERVANT #9: Shhh!!!

QUEEN: *(To Prince:)* That's easy enough!

(She grabs the shirt and throws it at the PRINCESS.)

QUEEN: Get to work!

(SERVANTS bring out the washtub and place it on a stool, center. PRINCESS puts the shirt inside and begins to scrub vigorously.)

PRINCESS: *(Singing off-key, from "The Merry Old Land Of Oz":)*
Scrub, scrub here,
Scrub, scrub there,
And a couple of lah-dee-dahs...

(She pulls out another shirt, which has been pre-set in the washtub, and holds it up. It is even more stained and dirty than the last. Everyone gasps with surprise.)

QUEEN: You IDIOT!!! Let *me* do it!

(She grabs the shirt and puts it in the washtub, scrubbing vigorously.)

QUEEN: You see, all it takes is a little elbow grease...

(She pulls out another prop shirt and holds it up – it's even more stained and dirty than the last one. Everyone gasps with surprise. BEAUTY casually strolls over to the washtub.)

BEAUTY: Let me try!

(She puts the shirt in the tub and scrubs gently, while humming the tune from "The Merry Old Land Of Oz." She pulls out a pristine white shirt and holds it up. All gasp with surprise.)

QUEEN & PRINCESS: *(Screaming, in agony.)* AAAHHH!!! You've broken the spell!

QUEEN: Now we'll be exiled from the Blue Planet!!!

(ALIENS enter, may be in spaceships.)

PRINCESS: The aliens are coming to take us away!

(ALIENS grab the QUEEN & PRINCESS, who are screaming and crying, and they all exit.)

SERVANTS: Hooray!!!
SERVANT #10: *(To PRINCE & BEAUTY:)* Will you stay with us here on our beautiful, Blue Planet?
BEAUTY: What's the name of this planet?
SERVANT #11: It's called Earth!
BEAUTY & PRINCE: We'll stay!
SERVANTS: Hooray!!!

(MUSIC BEGINS: optional song/dance. LIGHTS DOWN.)

ALL: The end!!!

APPENDIX A: VOCABULARY LIST OF FOREIGN LANGUAGE
(Not applicable)

APPENDIX B: SETS

SETS LIST

MOTHER & FATHER'S HOUSE:
> door – may be an already existing door, a curtain, or part of interior wall
> interior wall, freestanding – poor on one side, wealthy on the other
> chairs, table and/or pillows (optional)

BEAR'S CASTLE:
> bed, possibly with canopy
> chair
> exterior wall – freestanding wall, or curtain
> interior wall (optional; could be same as exterior wall)

OUTER SPACE:
> no sets are needed, but there should be several interesting locations around the performance space, possibly including levels, such as large, sturdy tables.
> backdrop (optional)

QUEEN'S CASTLE:
> exterior wall, with window (can use same as for Bear's castle)
> bed
> chair
> bedroom interior wall (optional)
> entrance to castle (optional – can be pantomimed)
> castle interior wall (optional)
> bush or other freestanding set for Beauty to hide behind (optional)

HOW TO MAKE THE SETS

FREESTANDING WALLS (for interior and exterior walls for Mother & Father's house, Bear's castle, and Queen's castle)
- very large, cardboard box
- cardboard cutting knife
- scissors
- heavy butcher paper
- tape or glue

- markers, crayons or paint with brushes
- colored paper or fabric (optional)

Cut box to create a freestanding wall with accordion folds. To make a window, draw a large square on the cardboard, with a vertical line down the middle. Cut this center line and across the top and bottom of square. Fold back the cardboard to make a window that opens and closes. Cut butcher paper to size of the wall. Tape or glue paper to wall, including both sides if the set will be reversed and including the window (if cardboard is plain white, you can eliminate this step). Draw picture of the set on the wall with markers, crayons ,or paint. Colored paper or fabric can also be used to decorate the wall, using glue or tape.

NOTE: if a door is part of the set, simply fold back one end of the wall so that it can open and shut. Don't cut the door from the center of the wall because the cardboard won't be strong enough to hold it up over time.

LANDSCAPE BACKDROP
- heavy butcher paper
- markers, crayons or paint with brushes
- sturdy tape
- scissors
- cut butcher paper to fit across upstage wall

Draw scenes of outer space with markers, crayons, or paint. Make sure the artists understand which end is up and that drawings must be large enough to be seen from the audience. Tape to wall.

APPENDIX C: PROPS
PROPS LIST

Small Backpack – with room for apple, carding-comb and spinning wheel
Silver Bell
Candle with Matches or Lighter (or use battery-operated candle)
Spaceships – for Old Women and possibly Aliens
Golden Apple
Golden Carding Comb
Golden Spinning Wheel
Princess's Giant Nose (see Costumes)
Goblet
Giant Handkerchief – for Princess
Wedding Decorations (optional) – streamers, balloons, and so forth
Washtub (large and deep so that shirts inside are not visible to audience; may have a sign on it reading: "Royal Washtub")
Stool or Chair (for washtub)
4 Shirts: one clean and white; another with three stains; the other two very stained, one more than the other

HOW TO MAKE THE PROPS

SPACE SHIPS
- very large cardboard box
- and/or child's wagon
- cardboard cutting tool, as needed
- rope pulleys, as needed
- decorations, as needed
- butcher paper, scissors, glue
- markers, crayons, or paint with brushes
- glitter, glue
- colored construction paper, scissors, glue

Spaceships can be decorated boxes with the bottoms cut out so that actors can walk inside while holding up the sides with their hands. This type of spaceship could also be operated by an actor who is on hands and knees inside the box and who propels it by pushing it forward as they crawl. Spaceships could also be constructed using a child's wagon that is either propelled by the feet, pulled by other actors, or pulled by a rope from backstage. Anything goes – give the actors time and freedom to invent and decorate their spaceships. Spaceships could also be replaced with "Space Horses," dressed in fanciful costumes, who "carry" Beauty on their backs by having her stand behind them with her hands on their shoulders while they gallop across the galaxies.

APPENDIX D: COSTUMES

BEAUTY, MOTHER, FATHER & CHILDREN: both poor and wealthy clothes – shirts & pants or skirts, or space suits. Beauty's rich dress should be easy to put on and take off swiftly and should include a pocket for the candle.

WHITE BEAR/PRINCE: white, royal outfit of pants & shirt or space suit, with bear mask and furry cloak that are easy to put on and take off swiftly

OLD WOMEN/MEN: pants & shirts or skirts, or space suits

WINDS: colored pants & shirts or leotards & tights, with colored scarves attached; or other, fanciful creation, easy to move in

QUEEN & PRINCESS: royal dresses or space-age creations. Princess has an absurdly long nose. In the last scene, Princess will wear a wedding dress, or at least veil, which should be easy to put on swiftly.

SERVANTS: pants & shirts or skirts, or space-age creations

APPENDIX E: SOUND & MUSIC

SOUND:

    Door knocking: wood blocks

    Magic when Beauty's dress appears: chimes or bells

    Storm/Wind Storm: drums, percussion instruments, noise makers and/or
        tape recorded sound

    Spaceships: percussion instruments, noise makers, and so forth

    Castle Door bell: hand bell

MUSIC:

    (All music can be selected from tapes or CD's, or played live.)

    Bear's Theme

    Wind Themes: East, West, South, and North

    Princess' Wedding Music

    Celebration Song for the very end of the show

    Scene Change Music (optional)

FENG ZHEN-ZHU
"The Wind Pearl"
(China)

Here's an ancient tale from China that follows the classic formula of the hero/heroine on a journey of self-discovery. Like all great heroes, Ha-Xin bravely pursues knowledge and enlightenment ("grain"). Along the way he suffers hardship ("99 mountains and rivers"), meets magical helpers (Old Woman and Yiouta, God of the Mountain—a figure of nature), encounters danger and "evil" (Kepoulah, King of the Serpents), endures a setback (is turned into a dog), is ultimately saved by love (Lan Fang), and in his fulfillment (becoming human again and marrying Lan Fang) he is better able to help his community (brings grain seeds to Poula). And, like all the best folktales, the element of magic is vital to both the plot and the delightfulness of the story.

This script is great for a large cast for there are many roles and lots of opportunities for acting, dance & movement, and music. The play calls for a lot of choreographed movement and dance and is ideal for a collaboration with a choreographer. In addition, there are a lot of sound effects and music in this play. A music director can be included, along with a separate sound and music ensemble. The battles, marches, waterfall, chase scenes, magical effects, and the Basket Dance all need to be carefully planned and rehearsed, with magnificent results. As there are very few sets required for production, you can really focus your time on movement and music.

This play can be incorporated with a study of China, and the script includes some Chinese language and a Chinese song. The Latin alphabet spellings in this script are based on the Mainland China system for Latin spellings. Taiwan and Hong Kong have different systems for spelling Chinese with the Latin alphabet, the alphabet we use for English.

This play can also be integrated with a science unit on seeds and their growth.

RUNNING TIME OF SHOW: *(approximate)*
    25-30 minutes
REHEARSAL TIME NEEDED:
    15-20 hours (more for large cast)
OTHER PRODUCTION TIME NEEDED:
    3-6 hours
CAST SIZE:
    Minimum: 12, plus Narrator (except for Ha Xin, all actors can play several roles.)
    Maximum: 30-40 (There can be numerous People of Poula and Loujo, Bing, Wèi-Bing, Enemy Bing, Bandits and Waterfall.)
GENDER OF CHARACTERS:
    Ha Xin, King of Poula, Ken Pang, and Suitors of Loujo are played as males; Queen of Poula, Lan Fan, and Young Women of Loujo are played as females; all other characters can be played as either male or female.

CHARACTERS:
    NARRATOR
    HA XIN – Prince of Poula
    QUEEN OF POULA – Ha Xin's mother
    KING OF POULA – Ha Xin's father
    PEOPLE OF POULA
    TRAVELERS
    BING – soldiers of Poula
    HORSE – of Ha Xin
    BANDITS & ENEMY BING
    SNAKE
    TIGER
    OLD WOMAN / MAN OF THE MOUNTAIN
    WATER FALL (optional – played by several actors)
    YIOUTA – God of the Mountain
    KEPOULAH – King / Queen of the Serpents
    WÈI-BING – Serpent guards of Kepoulah
    KEN PANG – Chief of Loujo
    LAN FANG – daughter of Ken Pang
    YOUNG WOMEN – of Loujo
    SUITORS – of Loujo
    PEOPLE OF LOUJO
    POULA WOMAN / MAN

SCENE 1

(Setting: China long ago, in the palace of Poula. There need be no set except 2 thrones. A background set, such as an interior wall, is possible if it can be easily removed. Mountains, and so on, for Scene 2 can be already in place. LIGHTS UP.)

NARRATOR: A long time ago in China, in the region of Yu Shu, there was a kingdom named Poula, ruled by a wise and generous King and Queen.

(KING & QUEEN enter and sit on their thrones. PEOPLE OF POULA may enter – optional – during the following narration.)

NARRATOR: The people there were very happy but all they had to eat were sheep and cattle, for no grain grew in Poula. Not a single grain of corn, barley, or wheat had ever grown there! The only son of the King and Queen, Prince Ha Xin, was very intelligent and curious about the world. Whenever travelers came through Poula, he would listen to their tales and ask many questions.

(HA XIN & TRAVELERS enter, talking. If need be, there can be only one or two TRAVELERS, or several.)

TRAVELER #1: Where we come from, Prince Ha Xin, tall and healthy plants grow which produce an excellent grain!

TRAVELER #2: The grain can be ground and cooked for food and it tastes really good!

TRAVELER #3: We have pancakes...pasta...popcorn...

ALL TRAVELERS: YUMMM!!!

HA XIN: I wish all the people here could have this good grain! Where can I get it?

ALL TRAVELERS: In the Land of Yiouta, the God of the Mountain!

HA XIN: *(To KING & QUEEN:)* Mama, Bàbà, I want to got to Yiouta to get grain for our people!

KING: It's too dangerous!

QUEEN: You're our only son!

KING & QUEEN: DON'T GO!!!

HA XIN: But today is my sixteenth birthday and you said I could do anything I wanted!

KING: *(To QUEEN:)* We always give him what he wants!

QUEEN: *(To HA XIN:)* All right, you can go. But we will send our *bing*, our best soldiers with you!

HA XIN: *Xìe-xìe!* Thank you!

(LIGHTS DOWN. ALL exit. Change set: Remove thrones.)

SCENE 2

(Setting: Across the countryside of China, on the way to Yiouta, a few weeks later. Ideally there should be one or more mountains, made with tables and chairs, over which the actors can march up and down, as across mountains. One mountain will also be used for YIOUTA and if you use actors to play WATERFALL, there will need to be either a slide or jumping-off place for them. A landscape backdrop is optional. HA XIN & HORSE should lead the march in a designated pattern while each interruption can happen at a different location around the stage. LIGHTS UP. HA XIN & HORSE enter, followed by BING. HA XIN wears a pouch on a cord around his neck and a saber hung by his side.)

BING: *(Singing – to the tune of "99 Bottles of Beer":)*
99 mountains and rivers to cross,
99 mountains and rivers!
We follow our boss
as over we cross!
98 mountains and rivers to cross!

(They continue singing, ad nauseam, marching around in single file. One actor should be designated as song leader, to restart the song after each of the following interruptions. With each interruption, there are fewer and fewer BING and their marching and singing becomes increasingly exhausted and miserable. Suddenly, BANDITS rush out at them.)

BANDITS: *(Screaming.)* ATTACK!!! *(and so forth)*

BING: BANDITS!!! HELP! HELP! *(and so forth)*

(BANDITS & BING battle with lots of yelling and screaming and some of each falling dead. Remaining BANDITS drag the dead bodies offstage while remaining BING regroup.)

BING: *(Singing:)*
78 mountains and rivers to cross... *(and so forth)*

(They continue singing and marching until interrupted by the follow-ing: A SNAKE darts out at them, biting a BING on the leg.)

SNAKE: HSSSS!!!

A BING: AAHHH!!! A snake bit me!!!

(BING screams and dies in agony. SNAKE slithers away. Remaining BING resume their march. SNAKE or other actor drags dead body off-stage.)

BING: *(Singing:)*
43 mountains and rivers to cross...*(and so forth)*

(They continue singing and marching until interrupted by the follow-ing: ENEMY BING suddenly attack them. ALL battle with lots of yelling and screaming, some of each falling dead. Remaining ENEMY BING drag the dead bodies offstage while remaining BING regroup.)

BING: *(Singing:)*
22 mountains and rivers to cross...*(and so forth)*

(They continue singing and marching until interrupted by the follow-ing: a TIGER leaps out and kills one or two of them. TIGER exits. There is now only one BING left, besides HA XIN & HORSE. They resume marching while TIGER or other actor drags the dead body off-stage.)

BING: *(Singing – just barely:)*
7 mountains and rivers to cross...*(and so forth)*

BING: Oh, I'm so tired...I can't go on...any...longer...

(BING dies.)

HA XIN: *(Singing:)*
6 mountains and rivers to cross...*(and so forth)*

(HA XIN & HORSE exit. LIGHTS DOWN. DEAD BING exits.)

SCENE 3

(Setting: On the way to Yiouta, a few weeks later. OLD WOMAN enters – she may be spinning. LIGHTS UP. HA XIN & HORSE enter wearily.)

HA XIN: *(Singing:)*
    2 mountains and rivers to cross,
    2 mountains and rivers.
    We follow our boss...HEY! *I'm* the boss!

(They approach OLD WOMAN.)

HA XIN: *Ni hao!* Can you tell me how to get to the Land of Yiouta?
OLD WOMAN: *Ni hao,* Prince Ha Xin! What took you so long? Listen: At the foot of this mountain is a river. Follow the river to a waterfall and there call out the name of Yiouta three times. He will come!
HA XIN: *Xìe-xìe! Zài-jiàn!*
OLD WOMAN: *Zài-jiàn!*

(OLD WOMAN exits as HA XIN & HORSE continue on their way. YIOUTA & WATERFALL enter a large mountain set. YIOUTA is under or behind the WATERFALL, hidden from view for the time being. MUSIC OR SOUND EFFECTS: WATERFALL. HA XIN & HORSE approach them. MUSIC OR SOUND volume comes down and continues softly under the following dialogue.)

HA XIN: *(Calling out.)* HONORABLE YIOUTA! YIOUTA! YIOUTA!

(SOUND: DRUM BEATS. YIOUTA appears, magnificently, at the top of the mountain.)

YIOUTA: Who is calling me?!!
HA XIN: *Ni hao!* I am Prince Ha Xin. I've come to ask for seeds so that my people may have grain to eat!
YIOUTA: WHAT?!! GRAIN!!!

(YIOUTA laughs so hard that the mountain/waterfall shakes; SOUND: DRUM BEATS.)

YIOUTA: Only in the country of Kepoulah, the King of the Serpents, is there any grain!
HA XIN: Will Kepoulah give me some seeds?
YIOUTA: *GIVE* you seeds?!!

(YIOUTA laughs so hard that the mountain/waterfall shakes; SOUND: DRUM BEATS.)

YIOUTA: The King of the Serpents is cruel and stingy! Everyone who asks him for seeds he changes into a *gou*, a dog! Kepoulah *eats* dogs! *(Laughs.)* Does that frighten you, Ha Xin?

HA XIN: *Bù!* No! I'm not afraid! What must I do to get the seeds?

YIOUTA: You are very brave, Ha Xin! Or very foolish!

Each day at noon, Kepoulah goes to the lake to meet the King of the Dragons. While he's gone, his *wèi-bing,*, his guards, take a nap. While they sleep you can steal the grain seeds from under Kepoulah's throne! And here, take this with you!

(YIOUTA pantomimes giving HA XIN a tiny seed.)

YIOUTA: That is *Feng Zhen-zhu,* the Wind Pearl! When you're in trouble, put it in your mouth and you will be able to run as fast as the wind!

If Kepoulah changes you into a *gou,* put the Wind Pearl in your mouth and run fast toward the east until you meet a young woman with a pure heart who loves you. Only then will you be able to return to your country and become a man again!

HA XIN: *Xìe-xìe! Zaì-jiàn!*

YIOUTA: *Zaì-jiàn!*

(WATERFALL MUSIC OR SOUND volumes comes up as HA XIN & HORSE exit. LIGHTS DOWN. ALL exit. MUSIC ENDS. Change set: set up KEPOULAH'S palace; remove YIOUTA'S mountain, if needed.)

SCENE 4

(Setting: The palace of Kepoulah, a few days later. There is a large, golden throne, under which are sacks of grain. No other set is needed; interior walls and palace entrance sets are possible. Opposite the palace is a place to represent the cave from where HA XIN watches the palace, such as under a table or inside a large box on a tabletop. A few WÈI-BING enter and stand guard – some at the throne and some at the entrance to the palace. LIGHTS UP. HA XIN & HORSE enter nearby.)

NARRATOR: Ha Xin arrived in the land of Kepoulah, the King of the Serpents, and saw that Kepoulah's palace was on top of a mountain. Ha Xin sent his horse back to Poula.

HA XIN: *Xìe-xìe! Zaì-jiàn!*

(HORSE whinnies "Zài-jiàn!" and exits.)

NARRATOR: Ha Xin then found a cave on a hilltop just opposite the palace of Kepoulah, from where he could watch everything that went on there.

(HA XIN settles into his "cave" observation place.)

NARRATOR: Just as Yiouta had told him, at noon Kepoulah came out, accompanied by his *Wèi-bing*, and headed for the lake to meet the King of the Dragons.

(MUSIC BEGINS: KEPOULAH'S THEME. KEPOULAH and the rest of the WÈI-BING enter ceremoniously and then exit as if going to to the lake. MUSIC ENDS.)

A THRONE WÈI-BING: Is he gone yet?
A PALACE ENTRANCE WÈI-BING: *(Looking.)* Yes!
ALL WÈI-BING: Nap time!!!

(ALL lie down and go to sleep. HA XIN comes out of his cave and goes to the palace. He tiptoes past the WÈI-BING and goes to throne. He reaches into one of the large sacks under the throne and pantomimes filling his pouch with grain. Finally, he takes a handful of grain which he keeps in his hand while he sneaks past the sleeping WÈI-BING. When he is almost out the entrance he accidentally trips over one of the WÈI-BING who wakes up with a shout. ALL wake up, shouting and jumping up to chase HA XIN. HA XIN throws his handful of grain into their faces and in the ensuing battle, draws out his saber and kills several WÈI-BING. HA XIN manages to escape the palace just as KEPOULAH and his WÈI-BING enter from the lake. HA XIN doesn't see them and bumps right into KEPOULAH. The WÈI-BING quickly surround HA XIN. HA XIN crawls through their legs.)

HA XIN: *Feng Zhen-zhu!*

(He pantomimes pulling the seed from his pocket and popping it into his mouth. He begins to run but at that very moment KEPOULAH dramatically puts a spell on him. SOUND EFFECTS: THUNDER & LIGHTNING. HA XIN immediately turns into a dog. Barking, he runs offstage while SOUND EFFECTS CONTINUE and KEPOULAH & WÈI-BING shout at him, angry that he escaped.

LIGHTS DOWN. SOUND EFFECTS END. Change set: Remove KEPOULAH'S palace and set up Loujo.)

SCENE 5

(Setting: The land of Loujo, two years later. There is a freestanding wall decorated as green fields and flowers. Some paper or plastic flowers are stuck onto into the wall which can be easily pulled out by LAN FANG. The reverse side of the wall is decorated as fields of ripe grain. There need be no other set for Loujo; a backdrop set is possible. LIGHTS UP. HA XIN enters, as a dog, and lays down near the green fields set.)

NARRATOR: Two years passed and still Ha Xin remained in the shape of a yellow *gou*, a dog. He had come to the country of Loujo. Grain did not grow here either, but the land was beautiful, covered with green grass and flowers. Here the chief of all the tribes was Ken Pang. Ken Pang had three daughters, the youngest of which was Lan Fang, which means "Perfume of Orchids."

(LAN FANG enters. She plucks the flowers off the green fields set.)

NARRATOR: Lan Fang loved flowers and animals. Remembering the words of Yiouta, Ha Xin thought that Lan Fang might be the young woman with a pure heart who could save him. He decided to offer her his seeds of grain.

(HA XIN goes up to LAN FANG who pets him.)

LAN FANG: *Ni hao, gou!* What's in this pouch around your neck?

(She pantomimes pulling grain seeds out of his pouch.)

LAN FANG: ...Some kind of seeds...

(HA XIN pantomimes digging a hole in the ground.)

LAN FANG: Now you're digging...You want me to plant the seeds?

(HA XIN barks and LAN FANG pantomimes planting the seeds from the pouch in the ground. She hugs HA XIN.)

LAN FANG: What a smart *gou!*

(They exit.)

NARRATOR: From that moment on, Lan Fang and the yellow *gou* became best friends. She loved this *gou* who had brought her the beautiful golden grain that remained a secret between them. Each day they went together to see their precious grain grow and ripen.

(The green fields set is turned around to reveal a scene of fields of ripe grain.)

NARRATOR: It was now autumn and all the crops of Loujo were ripe. One night when the moon was full, Chief Ken Pang held a gala dance.

(KEN PANG & ALL PEOPLE OF LOUJO enter. YOUNG WOMEN carry baskets of fruit, others may carry food and drink props for the party. When LAN FANG enters, HA XIN trails after her and stays near her during the following scene, watching her with loving eyes.)

KEN PANG: *(Loudly.)* Good people of Loujo, let's celebrate our good harvest!
ALL: *(Shouting.)* Good harvest!!

(ALL move to positions for the Basket Dance during the following narration.)

NARRATOR: During this celebration the young, unmarried women of the tribes were able to choose a husband if they wanted to.
According to tradition, each of these young women danced carrying a basket of fruit in her arms. When she finished dancing, she was to offer the fruit to the one whom she chose for her husband.

(MUSIC BEGINS: Basket Dance. During the dance, each YOUNG WOMAN chooses a SUITOR until only LAN FANG is left. She dances up to several suitors but rejects all, much to their and her father's increasing annoyance.)

KEN PANG: Choose a husband, daughter! A rich one!

(LAN FANG continues to dance, while HA XIN trails after her.)

SUITOR #1: What kind of man does she want?
SUITOR #2: She seems to prefer that yellow *gou!*

(ALL laugh loudly. LAN FANG, filled with emotion, places her basket in front of HA XIN. MUSIC STOPS. ALL gasp and there is a moment of stunned silence. What she has done is extremely scandalous.)

KEN PANG: *(Angry.)* Lan Fang, you have dishonored our family by choosing a *gou* for a husband! Leave with it and never return to Loujo!

(LAN FANG, crying, leaves with HA XIN. ALL exit, whispering about the scandal. LAN FANG & HA XIN re-enter and stop by the grain fields set.)

HA XIN: Lan Fang, don't cry anymore!

LAN FANG: *(Shocked.)* You can speak?!!

HA XIN: I am a man, changed into a *gou* by Kepoulah, King of the Serpents!

LAN FANG: Can you change back into a man?

HA XIN: Only if I meet a young woman with a pure heart who loves me!

LAN FANG: But I love you!

HA XIN: Then you must harvest all this grain and put the seeds in my pouch!

(LAN FANG pantomimes quickly harvesting the grain and putting the seeds in his pouch during the following narration.)

NARRATOR: While Lan Fang harvested the grain, Ha Xin explained that he would walk back to Poula, planting the grain seeds all along the way. Lan Fang was to follow far behind him, following the trail of growing grain plants.

(HA XIN & LAN FANG exit.)

NARRATOR: And it was so. As he walked toward Poula, Ha Xin stopped every few steps and planted some seeds while Lan Fang, following far behind, was guided by the trail of sprouts and later, stems, and still later, clusters of golden grain that showed her the way to Ha Xin's homeland.

(LIGHTS DOWN. Change set: Remove grain set and set up palace of Poula.)

SCENE 5

(Setting: The palace of Poula, a few months later. LIGHTS UP. POULA WOMAN enters, some distance from the palace. LAN FANG enters.)

LAN FANG: Is this Poula?

POULA WOMAN: Yes!

LAN FANG: Have you seen a yellow *gou?*

POULA WOMAN: Yes, I saw him pass through the gates of the palace this morning!

LAN FANG: *Xìe-xìe! Zaì-jiàn!*

POULA WOMAN: *Zaì-jiàn!*

(LAN FANG continues toward palace as POULA WOMAN exits. HA XIN enters, barking and running toward her, as a dog. SOUND EFFECTS: HA XIN is suddenly transformed back into a man.)

LAN FANG: Ha Xin!!! You're a man again!

(They embrace and exit.)

NARRATOR: They were married that very evening. It was a magnificent wedding attended by all the people of Poula.

(ALL enter.)

NARRATOR: Prince Ha Xin and Princess Lan Fang lived a long and happy life together and their love was as beautiful as a jasmine flower.

(May have song/dance here, "Mài Lì Hwā" or other Chinese song.)

ALL: *Wán-le!* The end!

(LIGHTS DOWN.)

APPENDIX A: VOCABULARY LIST
OF FOREIGN LANGUAGE

CHINESE *(spelled with Latin alphabet)*	ENGLISH	PRONUNCIATION
bing	soldiers	bing
wèi-bing	guards	way-bing'
bù	no	boo
feng zhen-zhu	wind pearl	fong zhen-zhoo'
gou	dog	go-oo' <small>(raise voice slightly at end)</small>
mama / bàbà	mother / father	mah'-mah / bah'-bah
ni hao	hello	nee' how
wán-le	the end	wahn'-luh
xìe-xìe	thank you	shay'-shay
zài-jiàn	good-bye	dzeye-jyehn'

"Mài Lì Hwa" (song):

Hau yì dywe mei lì de mài lì hwa	Oh, what a beautiful jasmine flower	how yih dwah may lee duh mwah lee hwah

SETS LIST

PALACE OF POULA:
> 2 thrones
> interior wall (optional)

MOUNTAINS:
> 1-4 large tables
> chairs, slides or other access to tabletops (as needed)
> large, dark cloths, hung from tabletops (optional)
> slide (optional – for waterfall)
> landscape backdrop (optional)

PALACE OF KEPOULAH
> 1 golden throne
> interior wall (optional)
> palace entrance (optional)

LOUJO:
> free-standing wall of green fields / ripe grain fields
> landscape backdrop (optional)

HOW TO MAKE THE SETS

FREESTANDING WALLS *(for green fields/grain fields, palace interiors)*
- very large, cardboard box
- cardboard cutting knife
- scissors
- heavy butcher paper
- tape or glue
- colored paper or fabric (optional)
- markers, crayons or paint with brushes

Cut box to create a freestanding wall with accordion folds. Cut 2 pieces of butcher paper to size of the wall. Tape or glue paper to both sides of the wall (if cardboard is plain white, you can eliminate this step). Draw picture of the set on the wall with markers, crayons or paint. Colored paper or fabric can also be used to decorate the wall, using glue or tape.

THRONES
- 2 chairs
- fabric pieces
- sturdy tape
- junk jewelry
- safety pins

Drape the chairs with fabric. Tape securely on back and bottom of chairs. Pin jewelry along the top and sides of the chairs.

LANDSCAPE BACKDROP
- heavy butcher paper
- sturdy tape

- markers, crayons or paint with brushes
- scissors

Cut butcher paper to fit across upstage wall. Draw scenes with markers, crayons or paint. Make sure the artists understand which end is up and that drawings must be large enough to be seen from the audience. Tape to wall.

APPENDIX C: PROPS

PROPS LIST

Pouch, on a Cord
Sabers (for all battles; can be worn with a waist sash)
Drop Spindle, Yarn (optional – for Old Woman)
Large Sacks (stuffed, as if full of grain seeds)
Flowers (paper or plastic; stuck onto green fields set)
Large Baskets of Fruit (plastic or papier mâché)

HOW TO MAKE THE PROPS

SABERS
- big Styrofoam or heavy cardboard pieces
- duct tape
- cutting tool

Draw sword or saber shape on Styrofoam or cardboard and cut out. Completely cover with duct tape. If using cardboard, make sure it's very thick as lightweight cardboard will bend too easily during rehearsals.

PAPIER MACHÉ FRUIT
- newspaper and white paper
- bowl
- 1/2 liter salt
- paint (fruit colors)
- masking tape
- 5-1/2 kgs. flour
- water
- paintbrushes

Roll or wad the paper into balls of various sizes and shapes. The outside layer of paper should be white (so that newspaper print does not show through the final layer of paint). Tape to secure. In a bowl mix together flour, salt, and water to make a mix the consistency of pancake batter. Cut or rip newspaper or other paper into long strips. Dip each strip into the mix and wipe off any excess. Apply it to the fruit shapes until they are completely covered. Allow to dry for 2-4 days. Paint.

FLOWERS
- colored tissue or other paper (tissue is best)
- ruler
- clear tape
- scissors
- pencil
- green pipe cleaners

Measure and cut several squares of the paper, each approximately 8-10 cm square. Layer 3-4 squares one top of each other, with the points of the squares going in different directions. Place the eraser end of the pencil in the center of the squares and gather the paper around the pencil end. Remove the pencil, twist the paper center while fluffing out the edges of the squares. Tape the twisted paper point to the end of a pipe cleaner.

COSTUME LIST

HA XIN: Chinese costume, or plain pants & shirt with possibly a royal jacket or vest

LAN FANG & YOUNG WOMEN OF POULA: Chinese costumes or plain dress or skirt

KING & QUEEN OF POULA: Chinese costumes, or long, fancy robes

BING, WÈI-BING, ENEMY BING & BANDITS: plain, dark pants & shirts, with sashes (to hold sabers) and possibly tunics, helmets

HA XIN'S HORSE, TIGER & SNAKE: plain-colored pants & shirt or leotard & tights, with ears and tail added as needed.

OLD WOMAN / MAN, POULA WOMAN / MAN: Chinese costumes, or plain pants & shirt or skirt

YIOUTA: dark cape or robes, or other fanciful costume

KEPOULAH: Chinese costume or dark cape or robes

KEN PANG, TRAVELERS, SUITORS, PEOPLE OF POULA & LOUJO: Chinese costumes or plain pants & shirts or skirts

HOW TO MAKE COSTUMES

HELMETS

- 11" x 17" pieces of colored construction paper
- markers
- stapler
- glitter, glue

In Chinese history, soldiers' hats were quite intricate and various. Here is a simple paper hat which actors can then decorate as suits their fancy. Holding the paper lengthwise, bring together the tips of the top corners and staple to create a cone shape. Fold up the bottom portion of the paper outwards and staple as needed to secure. Decorate with markers, glitter, and so on.

HORSE & TIGER EARS

- colored construction paper
- scissors
- light cardboard, glue (opt.)
- markers, crayons, paint with brushes, (op.)
- pencil
- stapler
- fake fur, glue (opt.)

Draw and cut out shape of ears with pencil on paper. Cut long strips of the same color, approximately 4 cm wide and long enough to go around the actors' heads with a 2-3 centimeters of overlap. Staple ears to strips, and staple strips to fit snugly around the actors' heads. You may want to reinforce ears and strips with a cardboard backing. Decorate as needed with markers, crayons or paint.

HORSE & TIGER TAILS
- long strips, approx. 1 meter long, of colored chiffon or other light fabric
- scissors
- long, elastic strip or safety pins

Measure out three strips of fabric. Braid together and tie in a knot at either end. Tail is either pinned to back of actor's pants or tied to an elastic strip that is measured and tied to fit around actor's waist. The best place to pin the tail to pants is through belt loops. If you pin it directly to pants or shirt, it can rip the fabric if someone steps on the tail.

APPENDIX E: SOUND & MUSIC

SOUND:
      Battle scenes: crashing cymbals and pounding drums
      Waterfall (if not using music): wind chimes or bells
      Yiouta: drum & mallets or cymbal
      Kepoulah's Spell on Ha Xin: crashing cymbals, pounding drums
          and possibly other percussion instruments
      Ha Xin's becoming a man again: same as above

MUSIC:
      Song: "99 Mountains & Rivers To Cross" (included)
      Song: "Mài Lì Hwa" (included, optional)
      Waterfall Music: any flowing-type of music, played live or on tape or CD
      Kepoulah's Theme: any Chinese music or march, played live or on
          tape or CD
      Basket Dance: any Chinese dance music, played live or on tape or CD

99 MOUNTAINS & RIVERS

tune: "99 Bottles of Beer"

Nine - ty - nine mount- tains and ri - vers to cross,

nine - ty - nine mount- tains and ri - vers! We

fol - low our boss, as o - ver we cross!

Nine - ty - nine moun - tains and ri - vers to cross!

(etc., *ad nauseam*)

MÀ LÌ HWĀ
("Jasmin Flower")

Andante, legato   Chinese folk song

Hǎu yì dywě měi lì mà lì hwā.

fra - grant, beau- ti - ful all o - ver the branch,

smells good, white co - lor, ev - ery - one praised.

Won't you please let me pick you?

So you won't be un - der wind and rain, mà lì

hwā, mà lì hwā.

LA CULEBRA
"The Snake"
(Mexico)

This is an ancient story that comes from the Aztec culture, told to me by Maria Gillman. It has an interesting twist of logic and ethics and makes a case for animal rights. You can involve your cast in discussion by asking, "Who is 'right' in this story?"

This script includes a large Spanish vocabulary which is useful for integrating Spanish language studies with reading and social studies. Because this play is fairly simple to rehearse and produce, it's a good one for when you don't have a lot of preparation time, or can be used simply as a reading activity. There are very few characters but all characters can be played as small groups. See Appendix A for plural endings to the Spanish words.

In this tale, *Coyote* plays the sly "Trickster," a figure well-known as well in some North American Native traditions. In the Pacific Northwest, "Raven" plays a like figure, as does "Anansi the Spider" in tales from Ghana and Liberia (see *The Adventures of Anansi* in Volume I of this collection).

This is a very action-packed story—you will need a lot of room for *los animales* to chase each other around. It's interesting if *Campesino*, the farmer, has a variety of creative places from which to escape the jaws of *Coyote*, such as on tabletops, under chairs, and so forth. The route of the chase scenes can also be varied for interest. For an added twist, you can require the audience to follow along during the chase scenes, leading them all over your building.

RUNNING TIME OF SHOW *(approximate):*
15 minutes

REHEARSAL TIME NEEDED:
6-8 hours

OTHER PRODUCTION TIME NEEDED:
2-4 hours

CAST SIZE:
Minimum: 5, plus Abuela/Narrator (actors playing Nieto, Esposa and Perros can play other characters)
Maximum: 20-25 (all characters can be played as small groups – see Appendix A to change word endings to plural)

GENDER OF CHARACTERS:
Campesino is a male farmer and Esposa is his wife. Gallina is a hen. All other characters can be played as either female or male – see Appendix A to change gender of words.

CHARACTERS:
ABUELA / ABUELO (NARRATOR) – grandmother / grandfather
NIETO / NIETA – grandson / granddaughter
BURRO – donkey
GALLINA – chicken, hen
PERROS – dogs
CULEBRA – snake
CAMPESINO – farmer
COYOTE
ESPOSA – wife of the farmer

(Setting: A small farm in Mexico. There need not be a set but there will need to be places where CAMPESINO can escape COYOTE. A couple of sturdy tables can serve as house and barn, with cloth hanging down the front, and CAMPESINO can escape to the rooftops. A backdrop of a Mexican farm is optional. LIGHTS UP. BURRO, GALLINA & PERROS enter and stand around the barnyard. ABUELA enters and stands to one side, watching. NIETO enters and goes up to BURRO.)

NIETO: *¡Hola, Señor Burro! ¿Habla español?*
BURRO: Hee haw! Hee haw!
NIETO: *¡Hola, Señorita Gallina! ¿Habla español?*
GALLINA: Plock-plock-plock-plock-plu-PLOCK!
NIETO: *¡Hola, Perros! ¿Hablon español?*
PERROS: Woof! Woof!
NIETO: *(Frustrated.)* Doesn't anyone around here speak Spanish?!!

(ABUELA comes over to her.)

ABUELA: I do! *¡Hola, Nieto!* Hello, grandson!
NIETO: *¡Hola, Abuela!* Hello, Grandmother!
ABUELA: *Nieto,* did you know there was a time when nobody in Mexico spoke Spanish? When the Aztecs lived here they spoke a language called *Náhuatl.*
And before that, there was a time when humans and *los animales* spoke the same language. Would you like to talk with *los animales, Nieto?*
NIETO: *¡Sí! ¡Sí!*
ABUELA: You can learn a lot from *los animales.* When *los animales* were able to talk with the children, *los niños,* the children were a lot smarter. And more sensitive. Back then, *los niños* didn't ask for money in exchange for a favor. They were not demanding and did not throw tantrums. The snake, *La Culebra,* taught them these things. I will tell you a story about *La Culebra.* This happened a long time ago.

(ANIMALES exit. ABUELA stands to one side while NIETO either stands with her throughout the play or goes backstage in order to play another character.)

ABUELA: In a small town in *México* called *San Miguel Tejocote,* there once was a terrible windstorm.

(SOUND EFFECTS: WINDSTORM. CULEBRA enters and lies down, center, and a large tree trunk is placed over her. Another option is to have one or more actors be the tree trunk and lie on top of CULEBRA. SOUND EFFECTS END.)

ABUELA: Later that day, *El Campesino*, the farmer, was working on his land when he heard someone screaming.

(CAMPESINO enters, with hoe.)

CULEBRA: *(Screaming.) ¡Ay, socorro! ¡Ay, socorro!*

ABUELA: *La Culebra* was trapped under a tree trunk and would surely die if she was not released!

(CAMPESINO goes over to CULEBRA and lifts tree off of her. CULEBRA shakes off the splinters.)

CULEBRA: *¡Gracias!* ...Now I'm going to eat you!! *¡Te voy a comer!*

(CULEBRA chases CAMPESINO)

CAMPESINO: *¡Ay, socorro! ¡Ay, socorro!*

(CAMPESINO finds a safe place, such as on a rooftop.)

CAMPESINO: But I saved your life!

CULEBRA: *Sí,* but remember the old proverb: If you do a good deed, in return something bad will happen to you!

ABUELA: *El Campesino* tried to explain that *La Culebra* had it all wrong, that if you do good, then good will come back to you in return. But *La Culebra* would not agree and insisted on eating *El Campesino* in return for saving her life. They argued for some time, until finally they agreed to ask *tres animales,* three animals, for their opinions on this matter. If all agreed with *La Culebra,* then she would eat *El Campesino.* They walked around the farm until they found *un burro,* a donkey.

(BURRO enters and CAMPESINO & CULEBRA walk over to him.)

CAMPESINO & CULEBRA: *¡Hola, Señor Burro!*

BURRO: *¡Hola, Campesino! ¡Hola, Culebra!*

CAMPESINO & CULEBRA: Is it true that if you do a good deed, in return something bad will happen to you?

BURRO: *(Thinks a moment.)...¡Sí!* I've worked hard all my life but when I get old they will surely kill me for my skin. So, if you do a good deed, in return something bad will happen to you! At least that's so for *burros*.

CULEBRA: *¡Te voy a comer!*

CAMPESINO: *¡Ay, socorro! ¡Ay, socorro!*

(CULEBRA chases CAMPESINO and BURRO joins in the chase until CAMPESINO finds a safe place.)

CAMPESINO: But we still have two more *animales* to ask – that was the deal!

CULEBRA: *Sí.*

ABUELA: They continued on their way and after awhile they met *una gallina,* a chicken.

(GALLINA enters and the others walk over to her.)

CAMPESINO, CULEBRA & BURRO: *¡Hola, Señorita Gallina!*

GALLINA: *¡Hola, Campesino! ¡Hola, Culebra! ¡Hola, Burro!*

CAMPESINO, CULEBRA & BURRO: Is it true that if you do a good deed, in return something bad will happen to you?

GALLINA: *(Thinks a moment.)* ...*¡Sí!* I lay eggs everyday for people to eat. But when I get old they will surely kill me and make me into chicken soup! So if you do a good deed, in return something bad will happen to you. At least that's so for *gallinas.*

CULEBRA: *¡Te voy a comer!*

CAMPESINO: *¡Ay, socorro! ¡Ay, socorro!*

(CULEBRA chases CAMPESINO and BURRO & GALLINA join in the chase until CAMPESINO finds a safe place.)

CAMPESINO: But we still have one more *animale* to ask – that was the deal!

CULEBRA: *Sí.*

ABUELA: After while they met *un coyote,* a coyote.

(COYOTE enters and the others walk up to him.)

CAMPESINO, CULEBRA, BURRO & GALLINA: *¡Hola, Coyote!*

COYOTE: *¡Hola, Campesino! ¡Hola, Culebra! ¡Hola, Burro! ¡Hola, Gallina!*

CAMPESINO, CULEBRA, BURRO & GALLINA: Is it true that if you do a good deed, in return something bad will happen to you?

COYOTE: How would I know? Everyone knows *Coyote* never does a good deed!

ALL: But you have to decide! You're the last *animal!*

CULEBRA: Besides, I'm getting very hungry!

COYOTE: *(Thinks a moment.)* ...You must show me exactly how it was.

ABUELA: And so they went back and put the tree trunk on top of *La Culebra* just like it was before.

(They do so.)

COYOTE: *(To Culebra:)* Can you move now?

CULEBRA: No!

COYOTE: Are you sure?

CULEBRA: Of course I'm sure! I can't move!

COYOTE: Not even *un poco,* a little?

CULEBRA: No, not even *un poco!*

COYOTE: So now you're just like at the beginning – the good deed is undone. Therefore, you cannot eat him! *¿Sí?*

CULEBRA: *(Sighs, outsmarted.) Sí.*

ABUELA: Satisfied that the matter was solved, everyone went back to their business about the farm.

(BURRO & GALLINA exit.)

CAMPESINO: *(To Coyote:) ¡Gracias, Coyote!* You saved my life!

COYOTE: *(With false sweetness.)* Well, I believe we should all help each other in this world. Just look at me: I'm sick! I'm soooo sick and faint with hunger...But you can help me.

CAMPESINO: How?

COYOTE: Bring me *dos borregos,* two of your best sheep. When I eat them, I will feel better!

CAMPESINO: *¡Sí!*

(COYOTE exits while CAMPESINO goes to his house as ESPOSA enters. Meanwhile, CULEBRA can either exit or stay in place under the log until the end of the play.)

ABUELA: *El Campesino* went home and told his *esposa,* his wife, the whole story.

ESPOSA: You're crazy! *¡Estás loco!*

CAMPESINO: Just give *Coyote dos borregos!*

(CAMPESINO exits.)

ESPOSA: Those *coyotes* are tricky but I know how to deal with them! *(Calls out:) ¡Perros! ¡Perros!*

(PERROS enter, barking.)

PERROS: *¿Sí, Señora?*
ESPOSA: Get in this sack, *por favor.*
PERROS: *Sí, Señora.*

(PERROS get into the sack. CAMPESINO enters.)

ESPOSA: Here they are, *dos borregos!*
CAMPESINO: *¡Gracias!*

(ESPOSA exits but watches the following scene from a hiding place. COYOTE enters.)

CAMPESINO: Here they are, *dos borregos!*
COYOTE: *¡Gracias!*

(COYOTE opens the sack. PERROS jump out, barking and snapping and chase COYOTE.)

COYOTE: *¡Ay, socorro! ¡Ay, socorro!*

(COYOTE finds a safe place temporarily.)

COYOTE: *La Culebra* was right! I did a good deed for *El Campesino* and in return something bad happened to me!

(PERROS chase COYOTE offstage. ALL exit.)

ABUELA: And that, *Nieto,* is the end of the story of *La Culebra.*
NIETO: Is it true? If so, I will never do any good deeds!
ABUELA: No, no, that's not the way it works! You should always do good deeds – but you should never expect something in return. If you only do good in order to get something back, then you will be tricked like *El Coyote. ¿Comprendes?*
NIETO: *¡Sí! ¡Sí!*

(MUSIC BEGINS: "La Bamba" or other Mexican folksongs. ALL enter and sing/dance. MUSIC ENDS.)

ALL: *¡El fin!* The end!

(LIGHTS DOWN.)

APPENDIX A: VOCABULARY LIST OF FOREIGN LANGUAGE

SPANISH	ENGLISH	PRONUNCIATION
abuela / abuelo	grandmother / grandfather	ah-booeh'-la / ah-booeh'-lo
animales	animals	ah-nee-mah'-lehs
¡Ay, socorro!	Help!	eye' suh-ko'-ro! *
borregos	sheep	bo-ray'-goes * (soft "s")
burro, el (plural: los burros)	donkey	boo'-ro *
campesino, el (plural: los campesinos)	farmer	kahm-pah-see'-no
coyote, el (plural: los coyotes)	coyote	ko-jo'-tay
culebra, la (plural: los culebras)	snake	koo-lay'-brah
el fin	the end	el feen'
esposa, la (plural: las esposas)	wife	eh-spo'-sah
estás loco	you're crazy	eh-stahs' lo'-ko
gallina, la (plural: las gallinas)	chicken, hen	gah-djee'-nah
gracias	thank you	grah'-see-ahs * (soft "s")
¿Habla español?	Do you speak Spanish?	ahb'-lah es-pah-nyol'?
hola	hello	oh'-lah
la / el / las / los	the (feminine / masculine / feminine-plural / masculine-plural)	lah / el / lahs / lohs
México	Mexico	meh'-hee-ko
Náhuatl	(language of the Aztecs)	naw'-tl
nieto / nieta	grandson / granddaughter	nee-eh'-toe / nee-eh'-tah
perros, los	dogs	pair'-ros * (soft "s")
por favor	please	pour fah-vohr'
señor	Mr. or sir	see-nyor'
señora / señorita	Mrs. or madame / Miss	see-nyor'-ah / see-nyor-ee'-tah
sí	yes	see
San Miguel Tejocote	(name of a town)	sahn mee-gel' tah-ho-ko'-tay (hard "g")
una / un	a	oo'-nah / oon
un poco	a little	oon po'-ko

"La Bamba"(song)

Para bailar la bamba	In order to dance "La Bamba"	pah'-rah bye'-yah lah bahn'-bah
Se necesita	You need to have	say neh-seh-see'-tah
una poca de gracia¡	a little gracefulness	oo'-nah poh'-kah day grah'-see-yah
Y otra cosita,	And something else:	ee oh'-trah ko-see'-ta
ay arriba y arriba!	UPBEAT! Yahoo!	yah-ree'-bah, yah-ree'-bah
por ti seré	it's for you to be	por tee seh-rey'

* NOTE: roll the "r's"

SETS LIST

FARMHOUSE (optional)
BARN (optional)
LANDSCAPE BACKDROP (optional)

HOW TO MAKE THE SETS

FARMHOUSE & BARN
Option #1:
- 1 or more tables
- cloth
- strong tape

Hang cloth from tabletops to floor, downstage. Cloths can be painted as front of the building.

Option #2: (freestanding walls)
- very large, cardboard box
- cardboard cutting knife
- scissors
- heavy butcher paper
- markers, crayons or paint with brushes
- tape or glue
- colored paper or fabric (optional)

Cut box to create a freestanding wall with accordion folds. Cut a piece of butcher paper to size of the wall. Tape or glue paper to the wall, including any hatches (if cardboard is plain white, you can eliminate this step). Draw picture of the set on the wall with markers, crayons or paint. Colored paper or fabric can also be used to decorate the wall, using glue or tape.

LANDSCAPE BACKDROP
- heavy butcher paper
- sturdy tape
- markers, crayons or paint with brushes
- scissors

Cut butcher paper to fit across upstage wall. Draw scenes of the Mexican country-side with markers, crayons or paint. Make sure the artists understand which end is up and that drawings must be large enough to be seen from the audience. Tape to wall.

APPENDIX C: PROPS

PROPS LIST

Tree
Hoe
Large Sack (big enough for *Perros*)

HOW TO MAKE PROPS

TREE
- large piece of sturdy cardboard
- strong tape
- brown paint & brushes or marker
- brown and green construction paper
- cutting tool
- scissors
- glue

Cut cardboard to make large, long rectangle. Roll cardboard to make a tubular trunk and tape to secure. Use brown cardboard and add bark markings with markers, or paint the trunk. Branches, twigs and leaves can be made out of cardboard and colored paper and taped or glued to trunk.

APPENDIX D: COSTUMES

COSTUME LIST

NIETO, ABUELA, CAMPESINO & ESPOSA: traditional Mexican or Aztec clothing, or pants & shirt, skirt & blouse, or dress.
LOS ANIMALES: pants & shirt or leotard & tights in the color of their animal, with ears, tails and feathers added on as needed.

HOW TO MAKE THE COSTUMES

ANIMAL EARS
- colored construction paper
- scissors
- light cardboard, glue (opt.)
- markers, crayons, paint with brushes, (opt.)
- pencil
- stapler
- fake fur, glue (opt.)

Draw and cut out shape of animal ears with pencil on appropriate color of paper. Cut long strips of the same colors, approximately 4 cm wide and long enough to go around the actors' heads with a 2-3 centimeters of overlap. Staple ears to strips, and staple strips to fit snugly around the actors' heads. You may want to reinforce ears and strips with a cardboard backing. Decorate as needed with markers, crayons, paint or bits of fake fur.

ANIMAL TAILS
- long strips, approx. 1 meter long, of colored chiffon or other light fabric
- scissors
- long, elastic strip or safety pins

Measure out three strips of fabric. Braid together and tie in a knot at either end. Tail is either pinned to back of actor's pants or tied to an elastic strip that is measured and tied to fit around actor's waist. The best place to pin the tail to pants is through belt loops. If you pin it directly to pants or shirt, it can rip the fabric if someone steps on the tail.

FOR GALLINA:
- feathers
- tape
- long, elastic strip

Measure and tie the elastic to fit around the actor's waist. Tape the feathers to the back of the elastic. You can also do a similar thing around the actor's head.

APPENDIX E: SOUND & MUSIC

SOUND:
Wind storm: noisemakers or percussion instruments

MUSIC:
Song: *"La Bamba"* (included)
Other Mexican folksongs, played live or on tape or CD

LA BAMBA

LEGEND OF THE SEASONS
(Lushootseed Salish)

This story comes from the Lushootseed Salish, the Native American or "First People" of the Puget Sound region of Western Washington, near Seattle. This script is adapted from a transcription of a telling by Harry Moses in 1952. The wording has not been changed except for the sake of clarity. Fortunately, many Lushootseed tales have been recorded and preserved. See the introduction to *Da-Hoos-Whee'-Whee ("The Seal-Hunting Brothers")* and its Appendix F on Lushootseed Salish Culture, for more information on Lushootseed culture and oral tradition. Another Lushootseed tale, *Star Story,* is included in Volume I of this collection.

This story is about a "spirit journey" that the Young Man takes to find enlightenment and completion of his self (symbolized by his searching for and marrying the Island Woman). A "spirit journey" is when a person goes on a journey of self-discovery and comes back with the widsom of self-knowledge or spiritual insight. Spirit journeys are respected in the culture of the "First People" and many are recorded as stories. The other Lushootseed tale in the volume, Da-Hoos-Whee'-Whee, is also a metaphorical spirit journey.

The key number in this story is four. In the culture of the First Peoples living north of the present Snohomish-King County line, four is the traditional number used in stories, just as the number three is prominent in traditional tales from Europe. The Young Man even has four wives! In Lushootseed society of the past, men usually had more than one wife.

RUNNING TIME OF SHOW: *(approximate)*
 25-30 minutes
REHEARSAL TIME NEEDED:
 12-15 hours
OTHER PRODUCTION TIME NEEDED:
 2-4 hours
CAST SIZE:
 Minimum: 11, plus Narrator (except for Young Man, all other actors can play several roles)
 Maximum: 25-30 (there can be numerous Relatives and Villagers)
GENDER OF CHARACTERS:
 Relatives and Villagers can be played as either female or male; all other characters should be played as designated.

CHARACTERS:
 NARRATOR
 SIAB – the Head Man of the village
 YOUNG WOMAN – his daughter
 YOUNG MAN
 KOI'-YAH – mother of the Young Man
 BAHD – father of the Young Man
 RELATIVES – of the Young Man
 VILLAGERS
 ISLAND WOMAN
 COOK
 HOUSEKEEPER
 DISHWASHER
 OLD MAN
 1ST OLD WOMAN
 GRANDSON – of the First Old Woman
 3 BROTHERS
 2ND OLD WOMAN – Grandmother of the Months
 DECEMBER
 JANUARY
 FEBRUARY
 MARCH
 FIANCÉ – of Island Woman
 SERVANT

SCENE 1

(Setting: A Lushootseed village along Puget Sound, a long time ago. 2 or 3 large, sturdy tables are set upstage. They have plain, dark fabric hanging from the tabletop to the floor, downstage. For now they are the houses of the village and later they will be mountains. There may be a landscape backdrop. A large box is backstage. LIGHTS UP.)

NARRATOR: Many people lived there in a small village. The Head Man, *Siab,* of this village lived there in the middle. He had a young daughter.

(SIAB & YOUNG WOMAN enter, from house.)

NARRATOR: Another family in the village had a son.

(YOUNG MAN enters. He and YOUNG WOMAN look at each other and smile.)

NARRATOR: This Young Man wanted to marry the daughter of the *Siab* but the *Siab* disapproved, because the boy and his family were poor.

(HEAD MAN notices YOUNG WOMAN & YOUNG MAN smiling at each other and angrily pulls her back into the house.)

NARRATOR: The young couple got together anyway!

(YOUNG WOMAN sneaks out of house and goes to YOUNG MAN.)

(MUSIC BEGINS: Drums. SIAB comes out of house, sees them together and chases them offstage. MUSIC ENDS.)

NARRATOR: The girl's father was furious! He planned a way to get rid of his son-in-law.

(SIAB enters with cedar box which he places center.)

NARRATOR: He built a big box made of *huh-pai',* cedar. And he put the Young Man in this box.

(MUSIC BEGINS: Drums. YOUNG MAN enters. SIAB chases him, captures him and forces him into the box. MUSIC ENDS.)

NARRATOR: It was early in the spring when this girl's father put the *huh-pai'* box into the water. It was about April.

(SIAB pushes the box into the water and it "floats" away – propelled by the actor inside – and exits. SIAB exits.)

NARRATOR: The box drifted now for one moon, a month. The Young Man's parents and relatives worried and looked for him.

(MUSIC BEGINS: Drums. KOI-YAH, BAHD & RELATIVES enter, looking all around for him then exit. MUSIC ENDS. LIGHTS DOWN.)

SCENE 2

(Setting: An island, a month later. The tables can remain as is. LIGHTS UP.)

NARRATOR: After the box drifted for one month, it came to the salt water and beached on the shore of a little island.

(Box with YOUNG MAN inside enters and stops, center.)

NARRATOR: A woman lived on this island with three other women – a housekeeper, a cook, and a dishwasher. The women had been on this island since the beginning of time.

(ISLAND WOMAN, HOUSEKEEPER, COOK & DISHWASHER enter.)

ISLAND WOMAN: Let's go for a walk together along the beach!
WOMEN: *Aiii!*

(They walk over to where the box is and are surprised to see it.)

HOUSEKEEPER: Look, a *huh-pai'* box!
ISLAND: Go get a tool to open it!

(One of them exits and returns with an axe. They chop the box and open the lid. The YOUNG MAN steps out.)

YOUNG MAN: *Tsi siab!*
WOMEN: *Siab!*
NARRATOR: He told them his story. The women felt sorry when he told them how he had been treated. He went home with them.

(ALL exit. LIGHTS DOWN.)

SCENE 3

(Setting: The same, a couple of months later. LIGHTS UP. WOMEN & YOUNG MAN enter.)

NARRATOR: The weather was getting warm now. It was about in July when the women told him:

COOK: Get yourself ready – you are going to go home to see your mother and father.

DISHWASHER: We must instruct you carefully because you are far away from your own territory.

NARRATOR: The women got ready to go along with him. They gave him some small nuts. Four of them.

WOMEN: Two are to be put in your left pocket and two in your right pocket!

(They give him the nuts and he puts them in his pockets.)

ISLAND WOMAN: You are not to show the nuts to your people until four days have passed!

(SOUND & LIGHT EFFECTS: The WOMEN twirl and magically disappear. YOUNG MAN is amazed. He exits. LIGHTS DOWN.)

SCENE 4

(Setting: The Lushootseed village, a few weeks later. LIGHTS UP.)

NARRATOR: After traveling for some time, the Young Man came to the place where the women had instructed him to beach the boat. Then he walked for a long time, but he finally came to his own village.

(YOUNG MAN enters. He wears a brilliant headpiece, with sun-rays on it.)

NARRATOR: His mother, *Koi'-yah* and father, *Bahd*, were there. They had grown old and had given up looking for their son.

(KOI'-YAH & BAHD enter from their house and YOUNG MAN comes up to them, but they can't see him because he is shining too brightly.)

NARRATOR: There stood something shining so bright, like the sun, that they couldn't see it.

Finally, as their eyes got accustomed to the light, they could see that this was a person.

KOI'-YAH & BAHD: Who are you?

YOUNG MAN: It's me, your son! I've come home!

KOI'-YAH & BAHD: It really is our lost son!

(YOUNG MAN stands with KOI'-YAH while BAHD hurries around the village, spreading the good news.)

BAHD: My son has come home! My son has come home!

(RELATIVES, VILLAGERS & SIAB enter and gather around YOUNG MAN. SIAB examines him closely.)

NARRATOR: The people all rushed over to share the happiness of the old people – even the *Siab!*

He examined the Young Man carefully and recognized him as the one he had put adrift in the tightly closed *huh-pai'* box. He was the same man, but yet he was different. He was so bright, he was shining!

SIAB: *(To YOUNG MAN:)* Now will you marry my daughter?

YOUNG MAN: *Whee!* No!

NARRATOR: Parents of other young women also asked him to be their son-in-law.

VILLAGER #1: Will you marry *my* daughter?

YOUNG MAN: *Whee!* No!

VILLAGER #2: Will you marry *my* daughter?

YOUNG MAN: *Whee!*

NARRATOR: The *Siab* coaxed him for three days to take his daughter, but still the Young Man said:

YOUNG MAN: *Whee!*

NARRATOR: Toward the end of the third day, the Young Man reached into his left pocket, took out a nut and rolled it over the house floor.

(He does so. SOUND & LIGHTS EFFECTS: HOUSEKEEPER magically appears, with brilliant headpiece or other costume brilliance. ALL are amazed.)

NARRATOR: When it quit rolling, there stood a beautiful young woman. She was shining so brightly that at first no one could look at her. The *Siab* looked at this beautiful woman and he asked the Young Man:

SIAB: Now will you marry my daughter?

YOUNG MAN: *Whee!*

NARRATOR: The Young Man reached into his pocket, took out another nut and rolled it over the floor.

(He does so. SOUND & LIGHTS EFFECTS: COOK magically appears, with brilliant headpiece or other costume brilliance.)

SIAB: *(To Young Man:)* Now will you marry my daughter?

YOUNG MAN: *Whee!*

(YOUNG MAN reaches into his pocket, pulls out another nut and rolls it across the floor. SOUND & LIGHT EFFECTS: DISHWASH-ER magically appears, like the others.)

NARRATOR: Why did the *Siab* want the son of the poor old man to marry his daughter when the Young Man already had three beautiful women?

(YOUNG MAN reaches into his pocket, pulls out a nut and rolls it across the floor. SOUND & LIGHT EFFECTS: ISLAND WOMAN magically appears, like the others.)

ISLAND WOMAN: *(Sternly, to Young Man:)* I instructed you that you were to wait four days before you revealed us to your people!

(SOUND & LIGHT EFFECTS: ALL ISLAND WOMEN magically disappear.)

NARRATOR: The village people felt sad for the Young man, but he just told them:

YOUNG MAN: Don't worry! I'm going to go and try to find my wives. *Huy!*

(He exits. LIGHTS DOWN.)

SCENE 5

(Setting: Mountain of OLD MAN and house of 1ST OLD WOMAN. The mountain is one of the tables – the OLD MAN sits on top, smoking a pipe – can use dry ice for special effect. There is a

stepladder, chair, or other access to the tabletop. On top of or in front of another table is the house of 1ST OLD WOMAN. There is a fire pit, three eating bowls, a water pitcher and 3 beans. LIGHTS UP. YOUNG MAN enters and goes up to OLD MAN.)

NARRATOR: He walked east for a long time until he came to a mountain. Near the top of the mountain he could see an old man.

YOUNG MAN: *Siab!*

OLD MAN: *Siab.* I've been sitting here since the world first began, smoking my pipe.

NARRATOR: The Old Man puffed on his long pipe and the Young Man could see clouds and fog rise from the bowl of his pipe. He walked on.

(YOUNG MAN leaves the OLD MAN and walks around performance space as 1ST OLD WOMAN enters and sits by the fire pit, sewing with a thimble. OLD MAN stays in place, smoking, until the end of the scene.)

NARRATOR: He walked for a long time until he came to an Old Woman who lived there in a big old house.

(YOUNG MAN walks up to 1ST OLD WOMAN.)

YOUNG MAN: *Tsi' siab!*

1ST OLD WOMAN: *Siab.*

YOUNG MAN: Are you all alone here?

1ST OLD WOMAN: *Whee!* I have a grandson who is out enjoying himself. Come stay with me for awhile and we can have supper together when my grandson comes home.

YOUNG MAN: *Aiii!*

(He sits down. 1ST OLD WOMAN acts out the following.)

NARRATOR: She had been sewing when the Young Man came in. Now she removed her thimble from her finger and she placed it on the fire. She poured some water into the thimble, took three beans and placed them into the water in the thimble. The Young Man watched this and wondered how three little beans, cooked in a thimble, could be enough for three people to eat for supper. The Old Woman could read the man's thoughts, but she said nothing.

When her Grandson came home, the Old Woman took the thimble from the fire and she put the food on the table.

(GRANDSON enters and sits. OLD WOMAN serves them from the thimble.)

NARRATOR: As they were eating, the Grandson told them that he had been in a horse race with many horses racing.

GRANDSON: My horse was a small one. We raced and jumped over a fire!

NARRATOR: As they talked they all ate the beans that were in the thimble. They ate and ate, and the thimble never got empty.

Now the Young Man told the Old Woman and her Grandson his story. He told them about being put into the *huh-pai'* box and everything that had happened to him. He told about the beautiful women and the nuts.

GRANDSON: I advise you to keep going in the direction that you have been traveling. *Huy!*

YOUNG MAN: *Huy!*

(YOUNG MAN exits. LIGHTS DOWN. ALL exit. Change set: Place a slide in front of one of the tables; take off fire pit and accompanying props and place skins on one tabletop.)

SCENE 6

(Setting: Mountain of the 3 BROTHERS and house of 2ND OLD WOMAN. One of the tables has a slide attached to it for the mountain. Another table is set with a pile of animal skins, for the house of 2ND OLD WOMAN. 3 BROTHERS enter on top of mountain, with coat. They are arguing over the coat and pulling it back and forth between them. LIGHTS UP. YOUNG MAN enters and approaches them.)

NARRATOR: He continued to walk until he came to three boys who were on top of a mountain. These boys had been quarreling since the beginning of time.

3 BROTHERS: *(Shouting and pulling coat.)* I want the coat! *Whee*, it's mine! *(and so on)*

YOUNG MAN: *Siab!*

3 BROTHERS: *Siab!*

YOUNG MAN: What are you doing?

BROTHER #1: Our eldest brother died and this coat belonged to him.

BROTHER #2: We are trying to decide who should have it.

BROTHER #3: This coat makes the one who wears it invisible!

NARRATOR: The Young Man told them they must earn the coat. He would take a ball to the top of the mountain and roll it. Whichever one of them touches it before it gets to the bottom is the one who will have the coat!

3 BROTHERS: *Aiii!*

(YOUNG MAN goes to top of mountain, gets a ball out of his pocket and rolls it down the mountain. 3 BROTHERS chase it but none touch it before it stops. They argue as they come back up the mountain, bringing the ball with them – improvise.)

3 BROTHERS: *(arguing)* I touched it! *Whee,* I touched! You didn't! *(and so on)*

YOUNG MAN: None of you touched it.

(Again, the YOUNG MAN rolls the ball down the mountain and the 3 BROTHERS chase it and yet none touches it before it stops. They argue as they come back up the mountain, bringing the ball with them.)

3 BROTHERS: *(Arguing.)* I touched it! *Whee,* I touched! You didn't! *(and so on)*

YOUNG MAN: None of you touched it.

(They repeat the procedure, as before. YOUNG MAN rolls the ball a fourth time.)

NARRATOR: Now, the fourth time the boys chased after the ball, the Young Man went over and put the coat on. He was invisible!

(YOUNG MAN puts on coat. 3 BROTHERS come back up the mountain with the ball.)

3 BROTHERS: Where is that man?

(They look all around for him, although he is standing right there. YOUNG MAN walks away. 3 BROTHERS exit. 2ND OLD WOMAN enters her house, in front of the table with the skins. She shivers with cold. YOUNG MAN walks over to her.)

NARRATOR: He walked until he came to an old lady living in a great big old house. She was cold and shivering.

YOUNG MAN: *Tsi siab!*

2ND OLD WOMAN: *Siab.*

YOUNG MAN: Are you all alone here?

2ND OLD WOMAN: *Whee!* I have four powerful grandsons, but they are not here right now. My grandsons are powerful! You will freeze when they come home. You had better hide over there in the corner, and I will cover you with these skins and you'll keep warm.

(YOUNG MAN climbs on top of the table and 2ND OLD WOMAN covers him with skins. They are both shivering with cold.)

2ND OLD WOMAN: My oldest grandson, December, will be home soon!

(DECEMBER enters.)

DECEMBER: *Kai'-yah,* grandmother, it smells like a person in here!

2ND OLD WOMAN: *Whee!* I'm all alone!

DECEMBER: *Kai'-yah,* I traveled from the north and as I came the ground froze, and the people got cold, and their fingers dropped off, and their ears dropped off, and they froze! The trees twisted and broke, and the water became ice, and it snowed!

(DECEMBER stands to one side.)

2ND OLD WOMAN: *(Shivering.)* My grandson, January, will be home soon!

(JANUARY enters.)

JANUARY: *Kai'-yah,* it smells like a person in here!

2ND OLD WOMAN: *Whee!* I'm all alone!

JANUARY: *Kai'-yah,* I twisted the trees and I broke them! I froze the people and the ground and the water!

(JANUARY stands next to DECEMBER.)

2ND OLD WOMAN: *(Shivering.)* My grandson, February, will be home soon!

(FEBRUARY enters. His hair stands up all over his head and he looks wild and mean.)

Legend of the Seasons 105

FEBRUARY: *Kai'-yah,* it smells like a person in here!

2ND OLD WOMAN: *Whee!* I'm all alone!

FEBRUARY: *Kai'-yah,* I made great freezing rains fall all over the people. Mountains slid into the rivers! Forests fell before me!

(FEBRUARY stands next to the others.)

2ND OLD WOMAN: My youngest grandson, March, is coming home! He is not dangerous.

(MARCH enters. 2ND OLD WOMAN stops shivering.)

MARCH: *Kai'-yah,* it smells like a person in here!

2ND OLD WOMAN: *Whee!* I'm all alone!

MARCH: *Kai'-yah,* I have been traveling for a long way behind my brothers. They have been killing people with the cold. I have been healing things with warmth. I thawed the ground so things can grow.

NARRATOR: The Young Man began to feel nice and warm.

(YOUNG MAN throws off the skins. MARCH looks at him.)

MARCH: Are you looking for something?

NARRATOR: March had such an understanding voice, the Young Man told him of all the troubles he had endured and of his travels as he searched for his wives.

March listened, and then he told the Young Man about a woman who was preparing to be married.

MARCH: There is going to be a big dinner and a party at that place. Hurry, and go in that direction. *(Points.) Huy!*

YOUNG MAN: *Huy!*

(YOUNG MAN exits. LIGHTS DOWN. Change set: Remove slide and skins.)

SCENE 7

(Setting: A village, a few days later. ISLAND WOMAN & ALL VIL-LAGERS enter and stand about, drinking tea and pantomiming chatting together. ISLAND WOMAN holds drinking cup and stands next to FIANCÉ while SERVANT stands nearby with pitcher. LIGHTS UP. YOUNG MAN enters, to one side, with coat.)

NARRATOR: The Young Man walked until finally he arrived at the village. He put on his magic coat.

(YOUNG MAN puts on coat and comes close to ISLAND WOMAN. Nobody sees him. SERVANT pours tea into her cup – pantomime.)

NARRATOR: He could see his wife from the island sitting there with a man she was about to marry. She was so pretty.

(YOUNG MAN reaches over ISLAND WOMAN'S shoulder and drinks her tea but she doesn't see him because he's invisible. She starts to drink and realizes her cup is empty.)

ISLAND WOMAN: Servant, you didn't give me any tea!
SERVANT: *Aiii!* I did!

(SERVANT fills her cup again. YOUNG MAN reaches over ISLAND WOMAN'S shoulder and drinks all her tea. ISLAND WOMAN starts to drink and realizes her cup is empty.)

ISLAND WOMAN: *(Irritated.)* Servant, you didn't give me any tea!
SERVANT: *Aiii!* I did!

(SERVANT fills her cup again. Again, YOUNG MAN drinks it and ISLAND WOMAN notices her cup is empty.)

ISLAND WOMAN: *(Angry.)* SERVANT!!! You didn't give me any tea!
SERVANT: *(Exasperated.) Aiii!!!* I did!
ISLAND WOMAN: Maybe my first husband is doing this to me. He is smart!
NARRATOR: She went into her sleeping room, and she came out with a very powerful tube which she put up to her eye.

(She gets out a small tube and looks all around through it.)

ISLAND WOMAN: I don't see anyone!

(She gets out another, larger tube and looks all around through it.)

ISLAND WOMAN: I don't see anyone!

(She gets out another, even larger tube and looks all around through it.)

ISLAND WOMAN: I don't see anyone!

(She gets out a ridiculously huge tube and looks all around through it. She sees the YOUNG MAN.)

ISLAND WOMAN: My husband!

(They embrace.)

NARRATOR: They went back to his people and they lived a happy life together. He found his wife in the month of April.

(May have song/dance here, "We All Fly Like Eagles," "The Earth Is Our Mother," or other song.)

ALL: *Hoi'-yah!* All is finished!

(LIGHTS DOWN.)

APPENDIX A: VOCABULARY LIST
OF FOREIGN LANGUAGE

LUSHOOTSEED	ENGLISH	PRONUNCIATION
aiii	yes	a'-eee
bahd	father	baad
hoi'-yah	the end	hoy'-awh
huh-pai'	cedar	huh-pie'ee
huy	good-bye	hoi
kai'-yah	grandmother	ki'-yah
koi'-yah	mother	koy'-ah
tsi siab	hello (said to females)	tsee' see-ab
siab	hello (said to males)	see'-ab
whee	no	whee (blow breath and pull in quickly at the end)

SETS LIST

2-3 large, sturdy tables
plain, dark cloths (hung from tabletops, down stage)
fire pit
slide
stepladder, chair, or other access to tabletop
landscape backdrop (optional)

HOW TO MAKE THE SETS

LANDSCAPE BACKDROP
- heavy butcher paper
- markers, crayons or paint with brushes
- sturdy tape
- scissors

Cut butcher paper to fit across upstage wall. Draw scenes of the Puget Sound landscape or seascape with markers, crayons or paint. Make sure the artists understand which end is up and that drawings must be large enough to be seen from the audience. Tape to wall.

APPENDIX C: PROPS

PROPS LIST

Cedar Box (use cardboard, painted brown with bottom cut out)
Axe
4 Nuts
Eating Bowls
Water/Tea Pitcher
3 Beans
Coat of Invisibility
Ball
Animal Skins (use fur coats, fake fur, or other cloths)
Drinking Cups
4 Tubes (graduating sizes)

HOW TO MAKE PROPS

AXE
- strong, thick cardboard or piece of sturdy foam

- cardboard cutting tool
- silver duct tape
- brown or black cloth or other wide tape

Draw the design for the tool on the cardboard or foam and cut out. The cardboard or foam must be very thick or the props won't survive rehearsals. Wrap the tape around the entire tool – silver duct tape for the stone blade and brown or black tape for the wooden handle.

TUBES
- toilet paper tube
- paper towel tube
- wrapping paper tube
- large piece of cardboard
- sturdy tape
- colored construction paper
- scissors
- glue
- markers, crayons of paint with brushes
- glitter

Roll the large piece of cardboard into a huge tube shape – the bigger the better, but the actor must be able to hold it up to her eye. Cover all tubes with colored paper or paint and decorate as desired with markers, crayons, paint, and/or glitter.

APPENDIX D: COSTUMES

COSTUME LIST

ALL CHARACTERS: traditional Lushootseed clothing or plain pants & shirts. Young Man must have pockets for nuts and brilliant headdress.

ALL ISLAND WOMEN: traditional Lushootseed clothing or plain pants & shirts or dresses, with colored scarves added. Each has a brilliant headdress and possibly some bright, shiny scarves for their reappearance in Scene 4.

OLD MAN: pants and shirt, with gray wig and long, gray beard

DECEMBER, JANUARY & FEBRUARY: white clothing, with paper or cloth snowflakes and icicles added to clothes and hair. They all are wild looking and may have long, white beards.

MARCH: Green clothing, with paper or cloth leaves added.

HOW TO MAKE THE COSTUMES

BRILLIANT HEADDRESSES (for Young Man and all Island Women)
- plastic headband
- gold, yellow and other, glittery pipe cleaners

Wrap pipe cleaners around headband so that they are secure and stick out, like rays. Make sure the ends of the pipe cleaners will not poke the actor's scalp.

APPENDIX E: SOUND & MUSIC

SOUND:

Magical effects when Island Women appear/disappear: percussion instruments

MUSIC:

Drums: played live or on tape or CD
Song: "Wearing our Long-Wing Feathers" (included)
Song: "We All Fly Like Eagles" (included, see Appendix E for *Da-Hoos-Wheé-Whee*)
Song: "The Earth Is Our Mother" (included, see Appendix E for *Da-Hoos-Wheé-Whee*)

APPENDIX F: LUSHOOTSEED SALISH CULTURE

(see Appendix F of *Da-Hoos-Whee'-Whee*)

WEARING OUR LONG-WING FEATHERS

MATAORA AND NIWAREKA IN THE UNDERWORLD
(Maori, New Zealand)

Here's a tale that's truly from "down under" – way down in the Underworld! This Maori myth explains how certain essential things came to be: the Maori warrior tattoo, called the *moko*; the beautiful designs and colors of Maori clothing; how *popoia* (owl) and *peka* (bat), night creatures who can see in the dark (both literally and as symbols of wisdom), came to live with us; and how the value of peace and gentleness was brought into the "Overworld", the world of the living, from *Rarohenga*, the Underworld.

This play presents the issue of domestic violence. Mataora loses his temper and hits Niwareka, his wife, who then reacts by running back to her home in *Rarohenga*. Throughout the course of the play, Mataora's love for Niwareka proves stronger than his temper and he returns from the Underworld a changed man who vows to be peaceful. He brings the nonviolent morals of *Rarohenga* to the Overworld in the designs of his *moko*, for a Maori man can be a strong warrior and still act with gentleness.

Domestic violence is an issue all-too familiar to many of our children, yet is generally a taboo subject in our schools. Presenting a play such as *Mataora* creates an opportunity for discussion about domestic violence and for kids to grapple with this issue psychologically, through drama and myth. The staged "hit" can be accomplished by having Mataora hold one hand up to Niwareka's face or arm and slapping that hand with his other hand, while Niwareka jumps back with a cry. It's even more realistic looking if the actors are turned slightly away from the audience.

The actors may be shy about touching each other, as when Mataora and Niwareka "rub noses" and later hug each other when reunited. The issue of touching is highly personal and I prefer to not press the matter as a matter of respect for children and their right to physical "boundaries." If the actors do feel uncomfortable with actually touching, I create stylized movements instead, such as making circles in the air with their noses while facing each other (nose rubbing) and making big, sweeping gestures with their arms toward each other (hugging).

Working with this script also opens up the opportunity to consider questions about what the Underworld is, where people go when they die, and other questions that move into the subject of religious beliefs (also taboo in many schools). The set for the Underworld can be whatever the kids fantasize it to be, as can the costumes for the spirits of *Rarohenga*.

There is the opportunity for both dance and drumming in this production. A nice addition to the production is to play a hand drum during scene changes and during dramatic moments.

RUNNING TIME OF SHOW *(approximate):*
 15-20 minutes
REHEARSAL TIME NEEDED:
 8-10 hours
OTHER PRODUCTION TIME NEEDED:
 3-5 hours
CAST SIZE:
 Minimum: 8, plus Narrator (Turehu can also play Guardian, Fantail, Young Man, Popoia and Peka; Niwareka's Sister can also play another role)
 Maximum: 20-25 (there can be numerous Turehu)
GENDER OF CHARACTERS:
 This is a myth about the creation of male warrior morals and tatoos as well as women's clothing designs in Maori culture, so the lead characters – Mataora, Niwareka and Ue-Tonga, as well as Young Man – should be played as designated. All other characters can be played as either male or female.

CHARACTERS:
 NARRATOR
 MATAORA – a young chief
 NIWAREKA – A Turehu woman
 TUREHU – Spirits of the Underworld
 NIWAREKA'S SISTER – also one of the Turehu
 GUARDIAN OF THE HOUSE OF 4 WINDS
 FANTAIL – a helping spirit
 UE-TONGA – Niwareka's father
 YOUNG MAN
 POPOIA – owl
 PEKA -bat

SCENE 1

(Setting: New Zealand, a long time ago. MATAORA'S hut is on one side of the stage, indicated by either a freestanding wall or a table with fabric hanging down the front. There is a fire pit in front of it. There may be a fishpond with fish nearby, or fish props backstage. Cooked food props are backstage. On the other side of the stage is the House of the 4 Winds, made of a sturdy table on top of which is a free-standing cardboard wall, decorated as the gateway to the Underworld. This wall can either open and close on the side like a gate or have a hatch cut into it, large enough for the actors to go through. On the Overworld side of the gate there is a slide, stepladder, or other way to access the tabletop. On the Underworld side of the gate a slide extends from the tabletop down to the Underworld. In lieu of a slide, some sort of creative way can be contrived to get from the tabletop to the floor. At the bottom of the slide is a tunnel which can be represented by either a table or some type of overhang, such as fabric draped over chairs, through which the actors can walk or crawl. The audience does not need to see the actors while they are in the tunnel. For now, there is a freestanding wall, decorated with a New Zealand landscape, set in front of the tunnel so that the audience does not see it yet. The reverse side of this wall is decorated as the Underworld and will be turned around when MATAORA goes down to the Underworld. LIGHTS UP.)

NARRATOR: Long ago there lived a great warrior chief of the Maori, the native people of New Zealand. His name was Mataora. One night Mataora came home from a party and went to sleep.

(MATAORA enters, lies down in front of his hut and closes his eyes. His face is painted with designs.)

NARRATOR: He dreamed about being in a fight to the death and being cheered by his people.

(MATAORA, asleep, makes fighting motions and may ad lib lines. MUSIC: DRUMS, CHIMES OR OTHER "MAGICAL" SOUNDS. NIWAREKA, NIWAREKA'S SISTER & other TUREHU enter from the Underworld and go through the gate to the Overworld. They gather around MATAORA. MUSIC ENDS. They stare at him, giggling loudly. He wakes up with a start.)

MATAORA: Who are you??!!

(The following TUREHU lines can be divided up among the actors as needed, including NIWAREKA and NIWAREKA'S SISTER.)

ALL TUREHU: *(Laughing.)* We are the *Turehu!*
TUREHU #1: We are from *Rarohenga*, the Underworld!
TUREHU #2: But what are you? Are you a god?
MATAORA: I am a man! Can't you see that for yourselves!
TUREHU #3: But you are not tattooed in the way of our people!
MATAORA: What do you mean? My face is tattooed!
TUREHU #4: Your *moko* is useless! It's only painted on!
TUREHU #5: A child could wipe yours off!

(A TUREHU wipes MATAORA'S face, smearing some but not all of his designs. The TUREHU laugh at him.)

MATAORA: *(Angry.)* What other way is there?
ALL TUREHU: You might find out one day! *(Giggle.)*
NARRATOR: Mataora, being a courteous host, asked them to sit down and share a meal. They agreed, but preferred to eat outside, not inside, his hut.

(TUREHU sit down around the fire pit while MATAORA goes into his hut.)

NARRATOR: Mataora was amazed for no one in his part of the country had ever before seen the *Turehu*. Mataora served them lots of good, cooked food.

(MATAORA returns with food, which he serves to the TUREHU who sniff it and look at it disdainfully.)

ALL TUREHU: This food is bad!!
NARRATOR: Mataora had given them his best food! Now he began to lose patience with these visitors from the Underworld.

(MATAORA grabs some of the food and eats it while the TUREHU gather around him, amazed.)

NARRATOR: He ate the food to show them that it was good and they crowded around him, staring and whispering amongst themselves:
ALL TUREHU: *(Stage whisper.)* He's still alive!!
NARRATOR: Some of them even pried his mouth open to see where the food had gone.

(One or two TUREHU open MATAORA'S mouth, and he pushes them away.)

MATAORA: *(Angry.)* What are you doing??!!
TUREHU #6: We *Turehu* only like raw food!

(MATAORA goes to pond or behind his hut while TUREHU sit by the fire pit again.)

NARRATOR: Mataora went to his little pond, caught several fresh fish and gave them, raw, to the spirits from the *Turehu*.

(He serves them the fish and the TUREHU eat them eagerly, laughing.)

NARRATOR: The *Turehu* laughed with delight and helped themselves. While they were eating Mataora had a chance to study them more closely.

(MATAORA walks around, observing them while they eat.)

NARRATOR: They were an elegant people, very tall, with thin noses, who wore waistmats of dried seaweed. They sat gracefully erect and laughed a lot. One young woman in particular caught Mataora's eye. She was very beautiful and just when he was thinking that he would like to get to know her better, she came over and sat next to him.

(NIWAREKA does so.)

NARRATOR: Mataora decided to entertain his guests with a dance, a dance worthy of a warrior and a chief.

(MUSIC BEGINS: Maori music or drums and percussion. MATAO-RA does a wild dance, jumping and whirling about. The TUREHU are delighted. MUSIC ENDS and MATAORA sits down.)

NARRATOR: When he was finished, the *Turehu* joined together in a stately dance, quite different from any other that Mataora had ever seen.

(MUSIC BEGINS: Maori music or drums and percussion. TUREHU dance: NIWAREKA takes the lead, weaving her feet in a small pattern, while the rest follow. They all join hands and weave in and out of each others' intertwined arms. MUSIC ENDS. TUREHU remain standing.)

NARRATOR: Mataora was so mesmerized by the beauty of their dance that he decided to ask them if he could choose a wife.

ALL TUREHU: Which one of us do you want?

(MATAORA stands and points to NIWAREKA who comes and stands next to him. They rub noses together.)

NARRATOR: As was the custom, they pressed their noses together. They were married right then and when the wedding was over Mataora's new bride said:

NIWAREKA: I am Niwareka, daughter of Ue-Tonga of the Underworld!

NARRATOR: They were very happy. Over the next few days the *Turehu* disappeared and went back to *Rarohenga*, the Underworld.

(MUSIC: TUREHU go through the gate, down the slide to the Underworld and exit. MATAORA & NIWAREKA go into hut. LIGHTS DOWN. MUSIC ENDS.)

SCENE 2

(Setting: Same, a few months later. LIGHTS UP.)

NARRATOR: Mataora and Niwareka grew to love each other very much. But something was wrong and they both knew it.

(MATAORA & NIWAREKA come out of the hut. MATAORA looks at the fire pit.)

MATAORA: *(Angry.)* Niwareka! You let the fire go out again!

(He strikes her. She cries out and runs away. During the following narration, she goes through the gate to the Underworld and exits. Meanwhile, MATAORA goes back into the hut.)

NARRATOR: Mataora's terrible temper frightened gentle Niwareka. The first time he hit her, she was devastated. She had never seen anyone being struck in the Underworld.
The next morning, Mataora discovered that Niwareka was gone.

(MATAORA comes out of his hut and looks around.)

NARRATOR: He remembered hitting her, but expected her to be

understanding about it. When a whole day passed and she didn't return, he became worried and decided to look for her. Only then did he begin to realize what a terrible thing he had done.

(MATAORA exits. LIGHTS DOWN. Change set: Replace MATAORA'S hut, fire pit and fish pond with the Underworld set. Turn around the landscape wall covering the tunnel, the reverse side of which is decorated as the Underworld, and place it to the side, such as in front of MATAORA'S hut, exposing the tunnel to the audience.)

SCENE 3

(Setting: The House of the Four Winds, as before, and the rest of the stage is now the Underworld. There is someplace from which the TUREHU can watch the tattooing while being hidden at first from the audience, such as from behind the freestanding wall. Backstage is MATAORA'S blood mask and NIWAREKA'S bundle. GUARDIAN enters and stands by the Gate. LIGHTS UP. MATAORA enters.)

NARRATOR: Mataora guessed that Niwareka had gone back to her home in *Rarohenga* and so he hurried in that direction, despite the dangers. He wanted to tell Niwareka how sorry he was, for he loved her very much.

(MATAORA enters, heading toward the House of Four Winds.)

NARRATOR: After awhile he came to the House of Four Winds where the spirits of the dead make their entrance to *Rarohenga*. Outside the House stood the Guardian of the Gate.

(MATAORA climbs the Overworld approach to the House.)

MATAORA: Have you seen a young woman pass this way?
GUARDIAN: Yes, a beautiful woman who was crying rushed past me awhile ago. You may follow if you have the courage!

(GUARDIAN opens the gate and MATAORA hesitates and then passes through. LIGHTS DOWN. MATAORA goes down the slide and into the tunnel, where he stumbles around in the darkness.)

NARRATOR: Mataora stumbled around in the dark of the tunnel to the Underworld until he saw a light and a fantail fluttering about. A fantail is always a good sign.

(FANTAIL enters with some type of light and shines it into the tunnel while dancing about.)

FANTAIL: Follow me! Follow me! I will keep you safe!
MATAORA: Have you seen a young woman pass this way?
FANTAIL: Yes! Her eyes were red and she was weeping.

(MATAORA, with the help of the FANTAIL'S light, makes it through to the end of the tunnel. When he emerges from the tunnel, LIGHTS UP. During the following narration, FANTAIL exits while MATAO-RA looks around the Underworld, amazed.)

NARRATOR: Soon Mataora came to the end of the tunnel and out into a new world where there was no sun but plenty of light, and no sky but a roof that seemed to be made out of rocks. Everything seemed to be bathed in light and birds were singing and there were trees and grass, just like in the real world. Mataora knew that this must be *Rarohenga*, the Underworld.

(UE-TONGA & YOUNG MAN enter. TUREHU watch from behind one of the sets, hidden or mostly hidden from the audience. YOUNG MAN lies down while UE-TONGA leans over him, tattooing his face with a fine chisel. YOUNG MAN either wears a mask of blood or has blood drips painted on his face. He occasionally groans with pain.)

NARRATOR: He saw a young man lying on the ground who seemed to be in agony while another, older, man was bending over him with a fine bone chisel which he was tapping into the face of the young man. Blood was streaming out of the wounds and yet the young man did not cry or shout.

(MATAORA goes up to them.)

MATAORA: I am Mataora!
UE-TONGA: *(Standing.)* I am Ue-Tonga!
MATAORA: What are you doing?
UE-TONGA: This is the way we do the *moko*, the tattoo.
MATAORA: No! My tattoo is the true *moko!* It's painted on!

(UE-TONGA disdainfully wipes Mataora's face with his hand, smearing his designs.)

MATAORA: *(Crying out, his hands to his face.)* Oh, no! My *moko!*

UE-TONGA: Your *moko* is useless! It's only painted on!

(TUREHU giggle and appear to the audience. MATAORA looks at them, distressed.)

NARRATOR: For a moment, Mataora thought he was back in his hut, dreaming about fighting to the death. The same faces were there, but he couldn't see Niwareka. Where was she? Ue-Tonga finished with the young man.

(YOUNG MAN rises, in agony, and exits.)

UE-TONGA: *(To MATAORA:)* Now I will put the real *moko* on your face!

(MATAORA lies down and UE-TONGA paints designs on his face during the following narration – use colored makeup sticks.)

NARRATOR: Ue-Tonga was a great master of the *moko*. The intricate patterns of twirls and swirls that he made on warrior's faces made them look both frightening and beautiful. Mataora closed his eyes, knowing that it was going to be very painful...and it was. Mataora could feel the drops of blood running down his face but he knew he must be brave because his new *moko* was special – it would stay on his face for the rest of his life.

As he lay there under the chisel, Mataora called out Niwareka's name over and over again, hoping that she would hear him. The wind carried his voice across the Rarohenga.

MATAORA: Niwareka!...Niwareka!...Niwareka!

NARRATOR: A younger sister of Niwareka heard the voice.

(NIWAREKA'S SISTER enters and dances around MATAORA. She goes to another part of the stage and brings NIWAREKA onto stage.)

SISTER: Niwareka, there's someone calling your name!

NIWAREKA: Where??!!

SISTER: He's lying over there on the ground, being tattooed by your father!

MATAORA: Niwareka!...Niwareka!...Niwareka!

(NIWAREKA goes to MATAORA. Meanwhile, UE-TONGA has placed a blood mask over MATAORA'S face. If you only have one blood mask, the YOUNG MAN'S mask can be re-used. MATAORA stands up, but cannot see NIWAREKA because his eyes are so swollen and bloody.)

NIWAREKA: Mataora, is it you under all that blood?

NARRATOR: They wept for joy because they were joined together again.

(MATAORA and NIWAREKA hug. LIGHTS DOWN. MATAORA takes off the blood mask and puts it backstage. He stands center stage, next to Niwareka, with his back to the audience.)

SCENE 4

(Setting: The same, a few days later.)

NARRATOR: When the *moko* wounds had healed, Mataora wanted to leave Rarohenga and return to the Overworld with Niwareka.

NIWAREKA: No, I think I will stay here.

MATAORA: *(Begging.)* Please, Niwareka!

UE-TONGA: Niwareka will stay here. She does not want to be attacked by you again!

MATAORA: I promise that from now on I will not be violent or lose my temper or strike Niwareka ever again!

(UE-TONGA & NIWAREKA turn away from him and pantomime discussing the matter for a moment, then turn back to MATAORA.)

UE-TONGA: We believe you. But the Overworld is a place of darkness. Be sure to take the light of *Rarohenga* back to your world!

(During the following narration, NIWAREKA'S SISTER gives NIWAREKA her bundle and NIWAREKA and MATAORA pantomime saying good-bye to all in the Underworld.)

NARRATOR: As Mataora and Niwareka set off on their journey back to the Overworld, Mataora knew that he was taking the good and gentle ways of the Underworld with him in the designs of his *moko*.

(NIWAREKA and MATAORA go to the tunnel. UE-TONGA, NIWAREKA'S SISTER, & TUREHU exit. FANTAIL enters.)

FANTAIL: You will need someone to guide you. Take *Popoia*, the owl, and *Peka*, the bat, with you.

(POPOIA & PEKA enter and fly around.)

NARRATOR: Mataora worried that *Popoia* and *Peka* would be chased by all the forest animals in the Overworld, but Fantail said:

FANTAIL: No, they'll be fine. They'll hide in the darkness of the night.

NARRATOR: *Popoia* and *Peka* showed them the way through the dark tunnel and that's how they came to be birds of the night in the Overworld.

(POPOIA, & PEKA lead MATAORA & NIWAREKA through the tunnel and up to the gate as GUARDIAN enters there. POPOIA & PEKA go through the gate, fly around the audience, and exit.)

NARRATOR: When they arrived at the House of the Four Winds, the Guardian of the Gate was waiting for them.

GUARDIAN: *(To Niwareka:)* What's that bundle you're carrying?

NIWAREKA: *(Flustered.)* Oh, nothing! It's only some clothes to wear in the Overworld!

GUARDIAN: *(Angry.)* You're trying to take something which should never leave *Rarohenga!* It's the garment of *Te Rangi-haupapa!* Show it to me!

(NIWAREKA reluctantly gives her bundle to the GUARDIAN who opens it and holds up a beautiful cloak covered with colorful, sparkling designs.)

NIWAREKA: I'd hoped to use it as a pattern for the cloaks of the women of the Overworld!

GUARDIAN: Because you tried to take something to the Overworld that belongs to the Underworld, the way will forever be closed. From now on, only the spirits of the dead may pass between the worlds!

(GUARDIAN gives NIWAREKA the cloak and she and MATAORA pass through the gate to the Overworld and exit.)

NARRATOR: And so, Mataora and Niwareka went on to spend their lives together quite happily.

It was Mataora who handed down the techniques and artistry of the *moko* from the Underworld and it was Niwareka who passed

on the patterns and colors used to weave beautiful skirts and cere-
monial cloaks.

ALL: The end!

APPENDIX A: VOCABULARY LIST OF FOREIGN LANGUAGE

MAORI	ENGLISH	PRONUNCIATION
Mataora		mah-tah-o'-rah (roll "r", "o" is soft)
moko	the art of tattooing	mo'-ko
Niwareka		nih-wah-reh'-kah (draw out "eh")
Peka	bat	peh'-keh
Popoia	owl	po-poy'-ah
Rarohenga	the Underworld	rah-row'-ehn-gah (hard "g")
Te Rangi-haupapa	a god or goddess of the Underworld	teh rahn'-gee- how-pa'-pa (hard "g")
Turehu	spirits of the Underworld	too-reh'-hoo
Ue-Tonga		oo'-eh-tone'-gah (hard "g")

SETS LIST

MATAORA'S HUT:
    freestanding wall, decorated as grass hut
    OR
    1 table, with fabric hanging down the front
    fire pit
    fish pond (optional – can use a piece of blue cloth)
    freestanding wall of New Zealand landscape (reverse side of
        Underworld set)

HOUSE OF THE 4 WINDS:
    1-2 sturdy tables
    slide, stepladder or other way up to tabletop from the Overworld
    slide or other way from tabletop down to the Underworld
    freestanding wall for gate

TUNNEL:
    (can be constructed with any of the following:)
    table or chairs draped with gauzelike fabric or other fabric
    gauzelike fabric or other fabric hung from ceiling or other overhang
    large cardboard box with both ends open

UNDERWORLD:
    freestanding wall, decorated as the Underworld (reverse side of New
        Zealand landscape)
    other decorated sets or tables draped with cloth (optional)

HOW TO MAKE THE SETS

FREESTANDING WALLS (for Mataora's hut, gate, New Zealand landscape and Underworld)
- very large, cardboard box
- cardboard cutting knife
- scissors
- heavy butcher paper
- tape or glue
- markers, crayons or paint with brushes
- colored paper or fabric (optional)
- paper cutter (optional)

Cut box to create a freestanding wall with accordion folds. For the gate: One end of the wall can fold open and shut or a hatch can be cut into the wall. To make a hatch, draw a square opening large enough for the actors to fit through from about the center of the wall to the floor. Cut the sides and fold up at the top or cut one side and the top and fold the other side. Cut butcher paper to size of the wall. Tape or glue paper to the wall, including the hatch (if cardboard is plain white, you can eliminate this step). Draw picture of the hut, gate, landscape or Underworld on the wall with markers, crayons or paint. Colored paper or fabric can also be used to decorate the wall, using glue or tape. To decorate as Mataora's grass hut, cut many long, thin strips of green, yellow and/or brown paper (easiest with paper cutter) and glue onto the wall by dabbing a bit of glue on the top of each strip.

FIRE PIT
- several cardboard paper towel tubes or other cardboard pieces, rolled liked logs
- flat piece of cardboard, approx. 30 cm. square
- red, orange and/or yellow tissue paper
- clear tape

Tape the tubes or other, log-shaped pieces of cardboard to the flat piece of cardboard. Tear the tissue paper into large pieces, stick them under and around the logs and tape with clear tape so that they jut up and out like flames.

PROPS LIST

Cooked Food – paper or plastic
Raw Fish – paper or plastic
Light – for Fantail, hand held or as part of costume
Chisel – cardboard
Make-Up Sticks
1-2 Blood Masks – papier mâché or other type of mask, covered with red
  tissue paper or paint
Cloak – decorated with colorful designs and glitter

COSTUME LIST

MATAORA, GUARDIAN, YOUNG MAN & UE-TONGA: traditional
  Maori dress, or plain, dark pants and shirts
NIWAREKA, NIWAREKA'S SISTER & TUREHU: traditional Maori dress
  or fanciful creations of Underworld fashions
FANTAIL: fanciful costume, including tail feathers. Can affix the light to cos-
  tume, such as hooking a small flashlight or bicycle light to waistband.
POPOIA: plain owl-colored pants & shirt or leotard & tights, with owl mask
PEKA: plain black pants & shirt or leotard and tights with bat wings

HOW TO MAKE THE COSTUMES

TAIL FEATHERS
  • colored paper, scissors
  OR
  • colored feathers
  OR
  • scraps of colored fabric
  • tape
  • 2 long, elastic strips
  • fabric cape, stapler (optional)
Measure and tie a piece of elastic to fit around the actor's waist. To make feathers,
draw feathers on paper and cut out, including fringe around the edges. Or, use real
feathers or scraps of fabric. Tape or tie the feathers or fabric scraps to the elastic so

that they hang down. The same thing can be done for a headdress and for arm pieces.

BAT WINGS
- black fabric
- scissors
- elastic strips
- stapler or needle and thread

Measure, cut and tie 6 elastic strips to fit around the actor's armpits/shoulders, elbows and wrists. Draw two large bat wings on the fabric and cut out. Staple or sew the wings to the elastic strips.

APPENDIX E: SOUND & MUSIC

MUSIC:
> For dances: Maori music, on tape, CD, or live, or live drums or other percussion instruments

NE HÖLMÖLÄISET
"The Silly Villagers"
Finland

This play is presented as a set of three, very silly stories. You can choose to do only one or two of them, or assign each story to a different group to perform. These stories require some special sets and props in order to play out the jokes – but the extra preparation time is well worth the hilarious effects. There is a slapstick humor to these stories that the actors – and audience – will really enjoy.

There are many Villager and Elder lines which can be distributed so that even with a large cast, everyone gets a line of their own. These lines can also be consolidated to fit a smaller cast. There's also a lot of Narrator lines in this script, which can be doled out among several actors as needed.

Several Finnish words are included in the script, as well as a Finnish folksong which can be added as a song or dance at the end.

A special thanks to the actors of the first Kids Action Theater production of *Ne Hölmöläiset* in 1989 who created the titles to these mini-plays: Kelly Day, Kathryn Krogstad, Renata Mann, Emmi Martini-Price, Anne Nylander, Jamie Pehoushek, Kent Truog, and Lily Wilson-Codega.

RUNNING TIME OF SHOW *(approximate)*:
    each story = 8-10 minutes
    all 3 stories = 25-30 minutes

REHEARSAL TIME NEEDED:
    each story = 5-6 hours
    all 3 stories = 15-20 hours

OTHER PRODUCTION TIME NEEDED:
    each story = 2-3 hours
    all 3 stories = 6-8 hours

CAST SIZE:
    Minimum: 7, plus Narrator
    Maximum: each story = 15-20; all 3 stories = 35-40 (each actor performs in one or two stories; if all actors are in all stories the stage action would be too chaotic.)

GENDER OF CHARACTERS:
    all characters can be played as either female or male

CHARACTERS:
    VILLAGERS – of Hölmola, Finland
    ELDERS – wise (?) persons of Hölmola
    MATTI / MAIJA – a stranger to Hölmola (male / female)

STORY #1: "The Sickle and the Sillies"

TOTAL LINES:
VILLAGERS = 9
ELDERS = 10

(Setting: The small, rural village of Hölmola, Finland, in the olden days. There may be a backdrop of the village and village houses, although they're not needed for the stories. Story #3 will require 1 or more large tables and a slide – for the time being these can be placed off to one side, or backstage. In one area of the stage there is a rye field set on which rye stalks can be raised and lowered from behind. For now, the rye stalks are upright. Backstage are rye stacks and all harvesting props. Backstage is a pole with a rope attached to one end. In another area of the stage is the lake, which does not need any set, or can have a backdrop. On the shore of the lake is a rowboat, large enough for all VILLAGERS & ELDERS in stories #1 and #3. LIGHTS UP.)

NARRATOR: Years ago, in a far-off corner of Finland, there was a little town called Hölmola. The people who lived there were known as *Ne Hölmöläiset*, which in Finnish means, "The Silly Villagers." *Ne Hölmöläiset* lived by themselves, never seeing or hearing anything of the outside world, and so they grew to be quite different and rather queer in their ways. They were simpleminded and above all, cautious. When it came to any important decisions, they would talk it over for weeks and months and even years before they could make up their minds to act. For example, when the folk in Hölmola first began to grow rye, they had the greatest trouble in the world deciding how to harvest it.

(VILLAGERS, including ELDERS, enter, pantomiming arguing, and stand around the rye field.)

NARRATOR: While they were talking and arguing about how the job should be done, their first crop grew ripe and wasted away.)

(Rye stalks fall down; SOUND: Slide whistle. VILLAGERS all groan and sit down, discouraged.)

NARRATOR: The next year, by the time the crop was ripe, the wise elders of the village had thought out a very careful plan.

(Rye stalks are pulled upright again; SOUND: Slide whistle.)

ELDER #1: *(Jumping up.)* This time, not a single grain is to be wasted!

ELDER #2: *(Jumping up.)* We shall divide the whole town into crews of seven people each to do the work of the harvest!

(VILLAGERS stand and act out the following.)

ELDER #3: First person bends the rye stalk over, one at a time!

(There is one stalk on the rye set which is not hooked up to the raising/lowering mechanism and this stalk is now held up by the actor. The following action is done with this rye stalk.)

ELDER #4: Second person holds a piece of wood under the stalk!

ELDER #5: Third person cuts the stalk with a sharp hatchet!

(SOUND: Wood blocks)

ELDER #6: Fourth person gathers the stalks into sheaves!

(Sheaves prop is brought out from behind rye set.)

ELDER #7: Fifth person binds them together!

ELDER #8: Sixth person carries the sheaves away!

ELDER #9: Seventh person builds them into a stack!

(One rye stack is brought onstage.)

NARRATOR: With this method, the villagers, working their hardest, could only harvest two sheaves a day. And so, most of the crop was lost again.

(Rye stalks fall down; SOUND: slide whistle. VILLAGERS all groan and begin to exit, discouraged.)

NARRATOR: A stranger named Matti happened to visit the town while this great harvesting work was going on and he was amazed.

(MATTI enters and watches the VILLAGERS exit.)

MATTI: *(To audience:)* I will teach Ne Hölmöläiset a thing or two!

(MATTI exits. SOME LIGHTS DOWN. Stage is lit by moonlight.)

NARRATOR: That night, while the Villagers were resting after their enormous labors, Matti went to the rye field.

(MATTI enters, with sickle, and begins to pantomime chopping the rye stalks.)

NARRATOR: Using a sickle, he cut and bound more rye in a few hours than the townsfolk had been able to harvest all week.

(Several more rye stacks are brought onstage while MATTI works. When finished, he drops the sickle beside one of the stacks and moves off to one side where he can watch the following from a distance, amused. MORE LIGHTS UP; SOUND: Rooster crowing. VILLAGERS, including ELDERS, enter and stand around, staring fearfully at the rye stacks.)

VILLAGER #1: What happened to our rye?!!
VILLAGER #2: It must be *taika,* magic!
VILLAGER #3: It's very dangerous *taika!*
VILLAGER #4: It must have been a *noita,* a magician who did this!
VILLAGER #5: *(Pointing to sickle.)* There's the evil *noita!*
VILLAGER #6: For our own safety, we must get rid of it!
VILLAGER #7: Let's drown it in the lake!
ALL: *Jaa!! Jaa!!*
VILLAGER #8: But how? It's too dangerous to touch it!
ELDER #10: Get a long pole!
ALL: *Jaa!! Jaa!!*

(They get a long pole which has a rope attached to one end which can be easily untied from the pole. The other end of the rope is tied with a slipknot loop. With much trepidation and improvised squeals of fear, they gingerly place the loop around the sickle and tighten it. Carrying the pole, they drag the sickle along the ground, making it bounce up and down while all cry out in great fear each time it bounces towards them.)

ALL: It's alive! It's alive! *Apua! Apua!* Help! Help! *(and so on)*

(In this manner, they travel to the lake and then stand around, pantomiming arguing.)

NARRATOR: When they arrived at the lake they spent an entire day standing around, arguing about how to get the sickle into the water. Finally, they agreed to take it out in a boat to the middle of the lake, tie a heavy rock to it and throw it overboard.

(As many as can fit into the boat climb in, gingerly holding the sickle

away from them, while someone brings a large rock with them. They row out into the middle of the lake and tie the rock to the rope. They attempt to throw the pole with sickle overboard but in so doing, the sickle gets hooked onto the side of the boat, making the boat and everyone in it tip dangerously to the side.)

VILLAGER # 9: The evil *noita* is trying to kill us!

ALL: *Apua! Apua! (and so on)*

(The boat tips over and all fall overboard, screaming and sputtering, frantically swimming to shore. When they reach the shore, they all lay there, panting.)

NARRATOR: The sickle was thus drowned and the whole town declared a month's holiday to celebrate their escape from the evil *noita*.

(May do song/dance here, "Kullan Ylistys" or other song. LIGHTS DOWN. ALL exit. Remove boat, rye field and rye stacks; bring the tree onstage.)

STORY #2: "The Light and the Light-headed"

TOTAL LINES:
VILLAGERS = 8
ELDERS = 16

(Setting: the village, as before. There is a large tree with branches, center stage. Set pieces for tupa *are backstage, with axes.)*

NARRATOR: When Matti next came to visit Hölmola, he found the villagers all in a great, big to-do. They had been arguing for over a year and this is how it all began: For as long as the oldest people of Hölmola could remember, *Ne Hölmöläiset* had always lived in *kotas,* houses shaped like wigwams. Lately they had, after much debate, decided to build for themselves *tupas,* simple, one-room log cabins.

(VILLAGERS, including ELDERS, enter. The VILLAGERS act out the following, with props:)

ELDER #1: First person cuts down the tree!

(Use axe and "fell" the tree; SOUND: wood blocks)

ELDER #2: Second person trims the branches!
ELDER #3: Third person peels off the bark!
ELDER #4: Fourth person measure the tree into lengths!

(Use string or measuring tape.)

ELDER #5: Fifth person cuts it into logs!

(Use axe and pantomime; SOUND: wood blocks.)

ELDER #6: Sixth and seventh persons carry the logs to the spot where the *tupa* is to be built!

(Take tree trunk backstage and return with tupa *walls, folded up and carried flat.)*

ELDER #7: Eighth person matches the logs at the ends so that they can be fitted together!
ELDER #8: Ninth and tenth persons set the logs in place for the walls!

(Raise the walls of the tupa.*)*

ELDER #9: Eleventh and twelfth persons lay the roof!
VILLAGER #1: We are building the *tupa* while the sun shines, so that it will always be filled with *valo*, light!
VILLAGER #2: We are trapping the *valo* in the walls of the *tupa* so that it will be light inside there forever!

(Work on the tupa *is completed. ALL step back to admire it.)*

VILLAGER #3: *Se on ihana!* It's lovely!

(Single file, they go into one end of the tupa *and come out the other side looking very distressed and confused because it's all dark inside.)*

VILLAGER #4: What happened?!!
VILLAGER #5: It's all dark inside!
VILLAGER #6: Where's all the *valo* we captured inside the walls?!!
VILLAGER #7: Someone must have let out all the *valo!*
VILLAGER #8: It was the evil *noita!*
ALL: Jaa!! Jaa!! The evil *noita!*
NARRATOR: They all sat down to think of another plan.

(ALL sit and pantomime arguing.)

NARRATOR: After months of arguing back and forth, they came to an agreement.

ELDER #10: *(Jumping up.)* We will carry the *valo* into the tupa!

ELDER #11: *(Jumping up.)* Go get some big sacks!

ALL: *(Jumping up.) Jaa!! Jaa!!*

> *(ALL rush offstage and come back with large sacks. They act out the following:)*

ELDER #12: Hold them open to the sun, to capture the *valo!*

ELDER #13: Now close them up tightly before the *valo* can escape!

ELDER #14: Now take the sacks into the *tupa* and open them up to release the *valo!*

> *(ALL do so – and come out again looking crestfallen.)*

ALL: It didn't work!

> *(ALL pantomime arguing. MATTI enters, carrying an axe.)*

MATTI: *Terve!* Hello!

> *(ALL eye him suspiciously.)*

MATTI: Now, I don't pretend to be wiser than anyone else, but long ago I discovered the secret of the sun! If you will pay me a thousands marks, I'll show you how to get the *valo* into your *tupa!*

> *(ALL huddle together, whispering, arguing, until they agree.)*

ALL: *(To MATTI:) Jaa, jaa!*

ELDER #15: Here's your thousand marks!

> *(Gives MATTI the money and he pockets it.)*

MATTI: Watch.

> *(He takes axe and hacks out a window in the wall; SOUND: Wood blocks. ALL peek inside the tupa.)*

ALL: *Valo! Valo!*

ELDER #16: Get the axes!

(ALL rush offstage and come back with axes. They begin to hack holes into the walls of the tupa.)

ALL: *Se on ihana! Se on ihana! (and so on)*

(They keep chopping furiously; SOUND: Wood blocks. In their frenzy the entire tupa collapses on top of them in a big heap. MATTI laughs and walks away.)

NARRATOR: After all their work had come to nothing, *Ne Hölmölaiset* decided that, all things considered, a *kota* is a better kind of house than a *tupa*.

(LIGHTS DOWN. ALL exit. Remove tupa set; set up rowboat, brush fire set and dead cow.)

STORY #3: "Idiots on Ice"

TOTAL LINES:
    VILLAGERS = 12
    ELDERS = 8

(Setting: The village, as before. On one side of the stage is the lake, with the rowboat and a freestanding brushfire set on one side and a dead cow on the other side – dead cow could be played by an actor. The frozen lake set is nearby, ready to be easily set up center stage. Backstage are several axes, some large sacks, enough bowls and spoons for all the actors and a huge spoon. LIGHTS UP. MATTI enters and approaches NARRATOR(S).)

MATTI: *Terve!*
NARRATOR: *(Suspiciously.)* Who are you?
MATTI: My name is Matti. Where are all *Ne Hölmölaiset?*
NARRATOR: Hmm...You look friendly enough. I'll tell you the story:
    It all started when a *lehmä*, a cow, was killed by a pack of wolves.
    The wolves had not had time to eat the *lehmä* before they were driven off by a herdsman.
    When the villagers heard about the dead *lehmä*, they rowed across the lake to where it lay.

(VILLAGERS, including ELDERS, enter. They get into the rowboat and row across the lake. They get out and stand around the dead cow.)

VILLAGER #1: What shall we do with the *lehmä?*

ELDER #1: *Sïna olet hupsu!* You are foolish! We shall cook it and eat it, of course!

VILLAGER #2: How will we cook the *lehmä?*

ELDER #2: *Sïna olet hupsu!* We shall cook it in a fire, of course!

VILLAGER #3: How will we make a fire big enough to cook the *lehmä?*

VILLAGER #4: We could wait for bolt of lightning to strike the *lehmä!*

ALL: *Jaa!! Jaa!*

ELDER #3: *Sïna olet hupsu!* The lightning would probably *burn* the *lehmä* and I like my meat cooked medium rare!

ALL: *(Discouraged.)* Oh.

VILLAGER #5: We could throw the *lehmä* into a volcano!

ALL: *Jaa! Jaa!*

ELDER #4: *Sïna olet hupsu!* There are no volcanos in Finland!

ALL: *(Discouraged.)* Oh.

NARRATOR: After many days of discussion, the *lehmä* started to smell very bad.

ALL: *(Holding their noses.)* PEE-U!!!

(Brushfire set begins to flame – as operated by backstage actors.)

ELDER #5: *(Pointing.)* Look, there's a brushfire burning on the other side of the lake. Let's take the *lehmä* over there!

ALL: *Jaa! Jaa!*

(ALL, still holding their noses, get into boat with the cow and row over to the brushfire that, meanwhile, is dying out. They get out of the boat and throw the cow in front of the fire that by now is almost out.)

NARRATOR: By the time they got there, however, the brushfire had almost burned out and the *lehmä* didn't cook all the way through.

(ALL pantomime picking up pieces of meat and eating it, and being disgusted because the meat is still raw.)

ALL: YUCK!!!

ELDER #3: I said I like it medium rare, not *raw!*

(ALL pantomime throwing the meat away. They pantomime arguing.)

NARRATOR: They argued about whose fault it was that they had nothing to eat. They argued for so long that the lake eventually became covered with a hard frost as winter set in.

(LIGHTS DOWN; ALL exit or change set. Frozen lake set is brought onstage; brushfire set, dead cow and rowboat can be taken offstage or left in place, out of the way. Frozen lake set consists of 1 or more large, sturdy tables, placed center stage. There needs to be enough room under the tables for all actors in this story to fit under. A slide is placed next to them, upstage. From the tabletops are hung icicles made of cloth or paper. Under the tables, attached to the legs and hung by strings from the underside of the tabletop, are fish and underwater plants. A white cloth is taped to the downstage edge of the tabletops and hangs all the way to the floor, so that the scene under the lake is hidden from view. It's best to not drape a cloth over the entire tabletop area because the actors could slip on it. LIGHTS UP. ALL enter and several climb on top of the table.)

VILLAGER #6: I'm so hungry I could eat a *lehmä!*

 VILLAGER #7: We already tried that!

ELDER #6: I know! Let's make *puuroa*, porridge!

ALL: *Jaa!! Jaa!!*

VILLAGER #8: But we don't have a kettle big enough to cook all the *puuroa* we want!

ELDER #7: We'll cut a big hole in the ice and make our *puuroa* in the lake!

ALL: *Jaa!! Jaa!!*

ELDER #8: Get the axes!!

ALL: *Jaa!! Jaa!!*

(Some of them exit and return with axes. They hand them to the actors on the tabletops who then pantomime chopping a big "hole" in the ice – where the top of the slide is. SOUND: Wood blocks. Meanwhile, others exit and return with large sacks and huge spoon. When the "hole" is cut, they hand the sacks to those on the tabletops who pantomime pouring the porridge mix into the hole. One person stirs the mix with the huge spoon. Others exit and return with bowls and spoons which they hand out to everyone.)

VILLAGER #8: *(On tabletop.)* I'll test to see if the *puuroa* is ready!

(She bends over the "hole" and with a cry, accidently slips on the ice and falls into the lake, sliding down the slide.)

NARRATOR: The others waited for her return. As time went by and still she did not return, they began to argue about why she stayed down there so long.

VILLAGER #9: The *puuroa* must be so good, she's sitting down there, on the bottom of the lake, stuffing herself, eating all of our shares!

VILLAGER #10: There'll be no *puuroa* left for the rest of us!

VILLAGER #11: I'll find her and bring her back!

(He bends over the "hole" and with a cry, accidently slips on the ice and falls into the lake, sliding down the slide.)

VILLAGER #12: Now they're *both* eating all our *puuroa!* I'll go see what's happening!

(She bends over the "hole" and with a cry, accidently slips on the ice and falls into the lake, sliding down the slide. One by one, ALL fall into the lake. Each can improvise a line and fall in with a dramatic flair. When all are in the lake, MATTI walks over and pulls up the white cloth up over the tabletop to reveal the scene of all the VIL-LAGERS & ELDERS, sitting or swimming, eating porridge from their bowls, and arguing with each other.)

MATTI: *(To audience.)* For all that I know, they're still there on the bottom of the lake, planning and arguing, and eating their fill of *puuroa*...and there they may still be to this very day.

(May do song/dance here, "Kulan Ylistys" or other Finnish folksong.)

ALL: *Loppu!* The end!

APPENDIX A: VOCABULARY LIST
OF FOREIGN LANGUAGE

FINNISH	ENGLISH	PRONUNCIATION
Apua!	Help!	ah'-poo-ah
Hölmöla / Ne Hölmölaiset	a fictional town in Finland/ its inhabitants; literally, "The Silly Villagers"	heu'-meu-lah / neh heu-meu-li'-set ("eu" pronunced as in German "ö")
jaa	yes	yaah
kota	small, wigwamlike house	ko'-tah
lehmä	cow	lehh'-mah (heavy "h"; "a" is pronounced as in "add")
loppu	the end	lah'-poo
marks	Finnish money	marks
Matti / Maija	a Finnish boy's / girl's name	mah'-tee / may'-ah
noita	magician, wizard	noy'-dtah
puuroa	porridge	poor'-oh-ah (roll "r"; long "oo")
Se on ihana!	It's lovely!	say ohn ee'-hahn-ah
Sïna olet hupsu!	You are foolish!	see'-nah o'-let hoops'-oo
taika	magic	dti'-gkah (soft "k")
terve	hello	tear'-vay (roll "r"; "tear" as in "to rip")
tupa	small, one-room log cabin	too'-pah
valo	light	vah'-lo

SETS LIST

ALL STORIES:
>   landscape backdrop (optional)
>   village houses (optional – can use freestanding walls, or tables covered
>   with cloth)

STORY #1:
>   rye field – freestanding set
>   several rye stacks
>   rowboat

STORY #2:
>   tupa (in pieces which can be assembled)
>   tree

STORY #3:
>   rowboat with oars
>   dead cow
>   brushfire set
>   frozen lake – 1 or more large, sturdy tables and a slide

HOW TO MAKE THE SETS

LANDSCAPE BACKDROP
- heavy butcher paper
- markers, crayons or paint with brushes
- sturdy tape
- scissors

Cut butcher paper to fit across upstage wall. Draw scenes of the Finnish country-side with markers, crayons or paint. Make sure the artists understand which end is up and that drawings must be large enough to be seen from the audience. Tape to wall.

FREESTANDING WALLS (for rye field, brush fire and village houses)
- very large, cardboard box
- cardboard cutting knife
- scissors
- heavy butcher paper
- tape or glue

- markers, crayons or paint with brushes
- colored paper or fabric (optional)
- paper cutter (optional)

Cut box to create a freestanding wall with accordian folds. Cut butcher paper to size of the wall. Tape or glue paper to one side of the wall, including the hatch (if cardboard is plain white, you can eliminate this step). Draw picture of the rye field, brushfire or village houses (kotas) on the wall with markers, crayons or paint. Colored paper or fabric can also be used to decorate the wall, using glue or tape.

RYE FIELD:
- gold or yellow colored paper, in pieces as long as the freestanding wall is high
- scissors
- cardboard cutting tool or knife
- long strips of brown or yellow fabric basting tape or other thin fabric strips
- long dowel or other length of wood, metal or plastic
- glue
- stapler

Glue the bottoms of the pieces of colored paper all along the length of the bottom of the freestanding wall. Allow to dry completely. With scissors, cut the paper into many long, thin strips. "Feather" the strips by clipping tiny little cuts along the edge of the strips, from about the center to the top of each strip. Gather up several small bunches of the strips, and around each bunch loosely wrap a strip of basting tape a few centimeters from the top of the bunch. Tie the tape loosely behind the bunch and staple the basting tape to the strips to secure it all together. With the cardboard cutting tool or knife cut little holes near the top of the freestanding wall and draw the ends of the basting tape through the holes. On the back side of the wall, tie the ends of the basting tape pieces around the dowel such that when the dowel, parallel to the floor, is raised up, the bunches of rye flop down to the floor and when the dowel is lowered to the floor, the rye is raised up. (This mechanism is operated by a backstage actor.) Make an extra small bunch of rye for use when the Elders describe their method of harvesting. This extra bunch should be glued to the bottom of the set along with the other stalks, perhaps in the middle of the set. It is loosely held together with a piece of basting tape, stapled to secure it, but it is not hooked up to the raising/lowering mechanism. You should be able to tuck it under another bunch of stalks until it's needed, or just leave it lying on the floor.

BRUSHFIRE:
- red, yellow and orange tissue paper
- cardboard cutting tool

Cut hatches in various places along the brushfire wall. To cut hatches, draw a square on the cardboard, large enough for the intended objects. Cut sides and bottom of square and fold up top to create a hatch door. Actors standing behind brushfire wall wave large pieces of colored tissue paper through the hatches to simulate fire.

RYE STACKS
Method #1: freestanding sets
- 4 or 5 large pieces of cardboard
- cardboard cutting tool
- duct tape
- butcher paper
- scissors
- glue
- markers, crayons or paint with brushes

Draw a dome-shaped rye stack on each piece of cardboard and cut it out. Lay each shape on butcher paper, trace around the edges and cut out an identical shape. Glue butcher paper to the cardboard (if using plain, white cardboard, you can eliminate this step). With markers, crayons or paint, decorate each as a stack of ripe rye stalks. Draw and cut out large, tall, right triangles out of remaining cardboard, as tall as the stack pieces, one for each stack. Bend back one edge of each triangle a few centimeters – this should be the longest side of the right angle – and tape securely to the back of the stack, the bent side perpendicular to the floor. This should make a prop which will hold the rye stack set upright.

Method #2: paper flipcharts
- freestanding wall (see above instructions) or other, short, freestanding wall
- butcher paper
- scissors
- tape
- markers, crayons or paint with brushes

Measure the butcher paper to cover the front side of the wall and cut out. Draw a rye field landscape on the paper with markers, crayons or paint and tape to the wall. On remaining butcher paper, draw 3 or 4 large, dome-shaped rye stacks, as tall as the wall, and color. At the top of each stack draw a long, vertical column and color as the sky. Cut out the stacks, including the column at the top. Tape the top of each column to the back side of the wall such that the stacks can be flipped over the top and overlaid on the landscape when Matti does his midnight harvesting.

ROWBOAT
- very large, cardboard box
- strong tape
- paint
- paint brushes

OR:
- butcher paper
- scissors
- glue
- markers or crayons

Fold and tape open both the top and bottom of the box. Paint the outside of the box. In lieu of paint, cover the outside of the ship with butcher paper and decorate with markers or crayons. Actors propel the boat by walking inside it while holding up the sides with their hands.

OARS
- 1 or 2 long poles, such as from a broom or mop
- 1 or 2 pieces of thick cardboard
- cardboard cutting tool
- tape
- paint, as needed

Draw a large circle, slightly oblong, on the cardboard, approximately 30 cm long. Use thick cardboard so it will not get easily bent. Draw a small column attached to the bottom of the circle, a few cm wide and long (for attaching to the pole), and cut out. Place the cardboard round near the top of the pole and wrap tape around the column, securing it to the pole. Paint as needed.

TUPA
- large, cardboard appliance box, brown
- 1 large, flat piece of cardboard, brown
- cardboard cutting tool
- sturdy tape, as needed
- brown paint or markers

Fold back and tape or cut off the top and bottom of the appliance box. Cut a straight, vertical line down the middle of one of the sides of the box. Spread open the sides of the box a little bit so that it stands as a three-sided, freestanding wall, with the middle side downstage, facing the audience, and the missing fourth side upstage. Actors will "enter and exit" the tupa by passing behind the back of it, as if going in one back door and out another one on the other side. The "roof" of the tupa is another, large, flat piece of cardboard which can be laid on top of the three-sided tupa. Draw and cut several hatches in the walls of the tupa. To cut hatches, several squares on the walls, each approximately 20 cm square. Cut sides and bottom of square and fold up top to create a hatch door. When the tupa is first set up, the hatches remain closed. When the Villagers go into a window-chopping frenzy, they hit their axes on the hatch squares which will open them up. With continued axe frenzy, the tupa will collapse on top of the actors as they pile into a big heap on the floor. Use paint or markers to draw wooden planks, wood knots, or nails in the tupa walls.

TREE
- large piece of brown cardboard
- 2 or 3 smaller pieces of brown cardboard
- cardboard cutting tool
- strong, brown tape
- large, brown paper shopping bags
- green construction paper
- glue

Cut and roll the large piece of cardboard to make a large cylinder that can stand upright (tree trunk). Cut and roll smaller pieces of cardboard to make smaller cylinders (branches). Cut out a few leaves out of the green paper and glue the tips to the branches. With cardboard cutting tool, make 2 or 3 small holes near the top of the trunk and insert the ends of the branches. The holes should be just the right size so that the branches will stay stuck in the trunk without falling out but can be pulled out easily. Rip the paper bags into long strips (bark). Dabble a tiny bit of glue here and there on the strips and stick them all over the trunk (the bark should be able to be pulled off fairly easily). Make extra bark strips so that the actors can practice this during rehearsals. If by performance time the trunk ends up with a lot of little torn paper pieces stuck all over it, all the better for looking like a trunk with bark.

DEAD COW
- 2 large pieces of butcher paper
- scissors
- markers, crayons or paint
- newspaper or other scrap paper
- stapler

Draw a large cow shape on one of the pieces of paper and cut out. Lay it on the other piece of paper, trace around the edges and cut out. With markers, crayons or paint, decorate one paper as a cow, then decorate the other as well on the opposite side (so that the two cow shapes are mirror-images of each other). Place the two papers together, matching sides, with cow decorations on the outside. Staple around the perimeters except for a length of about 30 cm or so. Stuff the cow with gently wadded-up newspaper or other, light, scrap paper. Finish stapling the last 30 cm of the edge.

FROZEN LAKE
- 1 or 2 large, sturdy tables
- 1 slide (can fold up one side of folded-leg table)
- large, white cloth

- white and colored construction paper
- scissors
- markers or crayons
- string
- tape

Draw and cut out of construction paper: long icicles, fish, other lake creatures, and lake plants. Decorate with markers or crayons as needed. Cut a few pieces of string and tape some of the fish and plants to the ends of the string pieces. Suspend these decorations from the underside of the tabletops and tape to secure. Other decorations can be taped to the table legs. Icicles are taped along the downstage edge of the tabletop. The large, white cloth is taped to the tabletop, downstage, and hangs to the floor, hiding the underside of the lake until Matti flips the cloth up.

APPENDIX C: PROPS

PROPS LIST

STORY #1:
    small piece of wood
    hatchet
    sheaf of rye stalks
    sickle
    long pole, with string attached
    large rock

STORY #2:
    measuring tape or string
    several large coins
    several large sacks (one for each actor)
    several axes (one for each actor)

STORY #3:
    several axes (use same as for Story #2)
    several large sacks (use same as for Story #2)
    huge spoon
    small bowls and spoons (one for each actor)

HOW TO MAKE THE PROPS

HATCHET, AXES & SICKLE
- strong, thick cardboard or pieces of sturdy foam
- cardboard cutting tool
- silver duct tape

- brown or black cloth or other wide tape

Draw the design for the tool on the cardboard or foam and cut out. The cardboard or foam must be very thick or the props won't survive rehearsals. Wrap the tape around the entire tool – silver duct tape for the metal parts and and brown or black tape for the handles.

SHEAF OF RYE STALKS

- long pieces of brown cardboard
- cardboard cutting tool
- yellow or gold construction paper
- scissors
- glue
- short length of wire or string

Cut several long, thin pieces of cardboard, approximately 60 cm long. Draw and cut oblong shapes out of yellow or gold paper, approximately 10 cm long. "Feather" the edges of the oblong shapes by clipping around the edges with scissors. Glue each oblong to the top of a cardboard strip.

LARGE ROCK

- large piece of white or colored paper
- newspapers
- masking tape
- paint, as needed
- stapler, as needed

Wad up the newspapers to make a large, rock shape and tape to secure. Cover the shape with white or rock-colored paper and staple or tape edges to secure. Paint as needed.

HUGE SPOON

- long pole, such as from a broom or mop
- piece of thick cardboard
- cardboard cutting tool
- tape
- paint, as needed

Draw a large circle, slightly oblong, on the cardboard, approximately 30 cm long (the bowl of the spoon). Use thick cardboard so it will not get easily bent. Draw a small column attached to the bottom of the circle, a few cm wide and long (for attaching to the pole), and cut out. Place the cardboard round near the top of the pole and wrap tape around the column, securing it to the pole. Paint as needed.

APPENDIX D: COSTUMES

ALL VILLAGERS, ELDERS, & MATTI: Traditional Finnish costumes, or plain pants & shirts or skirts. May add vests, jackets, hats, aprons, and so on

APPENDIX E: SOUND & MUSIC

SOUND:
    rye rising and falling (Story #1): slide whistle
    hatchet and axe chopping (all stories): wood blocks
    rooster crowing, live vocal or on tape or CD

MUSIC: (optional)
    "Kullan Ylistys" (included) or other Finnish folksong

KULLAN YLISTYS
("Praise To My Darling")

TRI ZLATE VLASY DEDA VSEVEDA
"The Three Golden Hairs of Grandfather Know All"
(Czech Republic)

This is another epic tale which has made it's way all over the map. Variations of it can be found as from Transylvania (a province of Romania), Bohemia (a region of Western Czechoslovakia), Finland, Germany, and surely many other regions as well. The story refers to the Black Sea, so it's likely to have traveled to the Middle East—or who knows, perhaps it originated there. When the hero floats down the river as a baby in a basket, we are reminded of the story of Moses from the Bible and when Deda Vseveda, Grandfather Know All, roars, "I smell man's flesh!," we think of the giant in "Jack and the Beanstalk." Tracing folktales is like a detective story—where did it begin, where did it travel to and how, and what will happen to this story next? By producing a play such as this with kids, the travel adventure of the folktale continues.

This production can include many actors, but it can also be done with a small, busy cast. The sets can be quite minimalist, although more complex sets can be included. There is no song/dance included with this script, but music can always be added, if desired, such as a celebration song at the end of the play. It's also possible to include a choreographed dance for the Fates.

This play is set in what is now called the Czech Republic. In that country both the Czech and Slovak languages are spoken, but for this script some Czech words are included. A production of this play can be integrated with a unit on Eastern Europe.

A "charcoal-burner" is a person who makes charcoal to be used in stoves. They do this by burning wood while limiting the supply of air, so that the more volatile ingredients burn away and the greater part of the carbon remains.

RUNNING TIME OF SHOW: *(approximately)*
   25-30 minutes
REHEARSAL TIME NEEDED:
   15-20 hours
OTHER PRODUCTION TIME NEEDED:
   4-6 hours
CAST SIZE:
   Minimum: 7, plus Narrator (Except for Plavacek, all other actors can play several roles; there need only be one Servant and one or two People.)
   Maximum: 25-30 (there can be numerous Servants and People)
GENDER OF CHARACTERS:
   First and Second Fates, Ferryman, Second and Third Krals, Beggar, Old Woman, Servants and People can be played as either female or male; all other roles should be played as designated.

CHARACTERS:
   NARRATOR
   PLAVACEK
   KRÁL – a king
   KRÁLOVNA – a queen
   PRINCESS – their daughter
   SERVANTS – for the Kral
   CHARCOAL BURNER – Plavacek's father
   CHARCOAL BURNER'S WIFE – Plavacek's mother
   1ST FATE
   2ND FATE
   3RD FATE
   FISHERMAN
   FISHERWOMAN
   FERRYMAN / WOMAN
   BEGGAR
   2ND KRÁL / KRÁLOVNA
   BLIND WOMAN / MAN
   3RD KRAL/ KRÁLOVNA
   PEOPLE – in the cities of the Krals
   DEDA VSEVEDA – Grandfather Know All, the Sun-King

SCENE 1

(Setting: Czech Republic, a long time ago. In one area of the stage is the forest and the cottage of the CHARCOAL-BURNER. In another area of the stage is the castle of the KRÁL. The castle will remain throughout the first 7 scenes of the play and again at the end. It should be situated off to one side and fairly easy to move on and offstage. It consists of 2 thrones and may have an interior wall. The cottage of the CHARCOAL-BURNER is made of a bed, chair, and a loft made of a sturdy table or other platform and either a stepladder or chair to provide access to the loft. Cottage may also have an interior wall. The door to the cottage can be pantomimed. CHARCOAL-BURNER'S WIFE lies in bed, while CHARCOAL-BURNER watches her anxiously from a chair nearby. LIGHTS UP.)

NARRATOR: In a faraway land which we now call the Czech Republic, there once lived a powerful *král*, which in the Czech language means "king." This *Král* loved to hunt wild beasts in *Cesky Les*, the Bohemian Forest. One day, while chasing a deer, he lost his way.

(KRÁL enters)

NARRATOR: He wandered about until, just as it was growing dark, he came to a charcoal-burner's small cottage.

(KRÁL knocks on door of cottage; SOUND: Door knocking. CHARCOAL-BURNER comes to the door.)

KRÁL: *Dobry den,* good day.
CHARCOAL-BURNER: *(Awed.) Dobry den, Král!*
KRÁL: Will you show me the way back to my castle? I'll give you good money.
CHARCOAL-BURNER: I'd be honored to serve you, but my wife is having a baby tonight and I can't leave her!
KRÁL: What a coincidence – my wife is also expecting a baby!
CHARCOAL-BURNER: Why don't you rest here tonight and I'll show you the way out of *Cesky Les* in the morning.
KRÁL: *Dekuji,* thank you.

(CHARCOAL-BURNER takes KRÁL inside and shows him the loft.)

KRÁL: *Dobrou noc,* good night!
CHARCOAL-BURNER: *Dobrou noc!*

(KRÁL gets into loft and CHARCOAL-BURNER checks on his wife and returns to his chair.)

NARRATOR: That night the Charcoal-Burner's wife gave birth to a healthy son.

(SOUND: Baby's cry. MUSIC BEGINS: Fates Theme. FATES enter and dance around the cottage. Each wears white and carries a lighted candle or white wand. KRÁL watches them from the loft while CHARCOAL-BURNER sleeps in his chair and his wife sleeps in bed with a baby doll. MUSIC comes DOWN under the following.)

1ST FATE: I bestow this boy with the gift of meeting great dangers!

2ND FATE: I grant him the power to escape all these dangers and live to an old age!

3RD FATE: I will bring to pass his marriage to the princess, born at this same hour, who is daughter of the *král* now sleeping in this cottage!

ALL FATES: One day this boy shall himself be the *král!*

(MUSIC comes UP. FATES exit. MUSIC ENDS. KRÁL paces in the loft, upset.)

NARRATOR: The *Král* knew that these were the Fates, the Hags of Destiny, and he was greatly disturbed by them. He lay awake all night, trying to think of a way to prevent the words of the Third Fate from coming true.

(LIGHTS DOWN. LIGHTS UP. CHARCOAL-BURNER wakes up and goes over to his wife.)

CHARCOAL-BURNER: AAAHHH!!! My beloved wife has died!

(Crying, he picks up the baby and holds it gently)

CHARCOAL-BURNER: Poor little *detatko!*, poor baby! What will you do now without your *matka,* your mother?

(KRÁL comes down from loft.)

KRÁL: Give *me* the *detatko!* I will see that he's always happy and that you have plenty of money!

CHARCOAL-BURNER: *(Dumfounded.)* You are too kind, good *Král! Dekuji!*

KRÁL: No need to thank me. Just show me the way to my castle!
CHARCOAL-BURNER: *Ano*, yes!

(LIGHTS DOWN.)

SCENE 2

(Setting: The castle of the KRÁL & KRÁLOVNA. There are 2 thrones and may also be an interior wall. LIGHTS UP. KRÁL enters from one side as SERVANT #1 enters from another side.)

SERVANT #1: *Dobry den, Král!* The *Královna* gave birth last night to a beautiful daughter!
KRÁL: *(Angry.)* She did!
SERVANT #1: *(Taken aback.)* I thought you would be pleased...
KRÁL: Servant, go at once to the cottage of the Charcoal-Burner in *Cesky Les*. Give him this money and take his *detatko* from him.

(KRÁL gives him some money.)

SERVANT #1: *Ano*, Král.
KRÁL: Then you must take the *detatko* and drown it in the river!
SERVANT #1: *(Shocked.)* Drown it?!! *Ne!*
KRÁL: Do as I say, or you'll come to the same end yourself!
SERVANT #1: *(Sadly.) Ano, Král.*

(They exit. LIGHTS DOWN. Change set: remove CHARCOAL-BURNER'S house and replace it with river and FISHERMAN'S hut.)

SCENE 3

(Setting: The river – it can be pantomimed, or lay a long, blue cloth on the floor. There is a fishing line or other clear string laid out on the river with a hook at the end for attaching to the basket. The other end will be pulled by someone backstage. SERVANT #1 enters with baby in the basket. He places the basket in the river at one end and attaches it to the hook.)

SERVANT #1: *(Sadly.) Na shledanou, detatko!* Farewell, little baby!

(Basket is slowly pulled up the river. SERVANT #1 watches it for a

moment then exits. FISHERMAN enters near the other end of the river. He sees the basket coming toward him.)

FISHERMAN: What is that floating in the river?

(He pulls the basket out of the river, detaching it from the hook. He looks inside.)

FISHERMAN: A *detatko!!!*

(FISHERMAN'S WIFE enters.)

FISHERMAN: Dear wife! Look what I found in the river!

(FISHERMAN gives the basket to her and she looks inside.)

FISHERMAN'S WIFE: A *detatko!!!*
FISHERMAN: We've always wished for a son and now the river has brought us one!
FISHERMAN'S WIFE: *Ano!* We shall name him Plavacek which means "floater" because he has floated to us on the river!

(LIGHTS DOWN. They exit, with basket.)

SCENE 4

(Setting: The same, 20 years later. LIGHTS UP.)

NARRATOR: Many years passed and Plavacek was happy with his foster parents. He helped them with their fishing business and played on the banks of the river as he grew into a handsome youth.
One day the *Král* chanced to pass by.

(KRAL enters from one side of the stage, carrying a small shoulder bag, while FISHERMAN & FISHERWOMAN enter from another side, may carry fishing nets.)

KRÁL: *Dobry den.*
FISHERMAN & FISHERWOMAN: *(Awed.) Dobry den, Král!*
KRÁL: I would like a drink of water.
FISHERWOMAN: *Ano! (Calls out.)* Plavacek!
PLAVACEK: *(From backstage.) Ano, Matka?*
FISHERWOMAN: Bring our guest a drink of water!

(PLAVACEK enters, with a cup which he gives to KRÁL. KRÁL drinks while looking at him closely. He speaks to FISHERMAN & FISHERWOMAN.)

KRÁL: What a fine young man! Is he your son?

FISHERMAN: *Ne.* Twenty years ago we fished him out of the river and have raised him as our own son!

KRÁL: Hmm...I need a messenger to carry a letter to the *Královna. (To Plavacek:)* Would you go for me?

PLAVACEK: *Ano!*

(KRÁL gets a paper and feather quill pen out of his bag and writes during the following.)

NARRATOR: The letter said: "Dear wife, have this lad put to death! He is my dangerous enemy!"

KRÁL: Take this to the castle.

(He folds letter and gives it to Plavacek.)

PLAVACEK: *Ano!*

(PLAVACEK exits. LIGHTS DOWN. ALL exit. Change set: Bring out cottage of the FATES.)

SCENE 5

(Setting: the cottage of the FATES. There are 3 chairs and a bed or sleeping mat and may also be an interior wall – can use the same as for CHARCOAL-BURNER'S cottage. LIGHTS UP. FATES enter from one side of the stage while PLAVACEK enters from another side.)

PLAVACEK: *Dobry den!*

FATES: *Dobry den,* Plavacek!

PLAVACEK: How did you know my name?!!

1ST FATE: We are your godmothers!

PLAVACEK: I've lost my way – can you show me the road to the *Král's* castle?

2ND FATE: *Ano.* But it's getting dark now – come rest in our cottage and we'll show you the way in the morning.

PLAVACEK: *Dekuji.*

(They go into the cottage. The FATES show him his bed.)

PLAVACEK: *Dobrou noc!*
FATES: *Dobrou noc!*

(PLAVACEK gets into bed and goes to sleep. MUSIC BEGINS: Fates Theme. The FATES watch him for a moment and then 1ST FATE pulls the letter out of his pocket and holds it up. 2ND FATE gets out another letter and they replace it with the one that PLAVACEK was carrying. FATES sit in their chairs and watch PLAVACEK. MUSIC ENDS. LIGHTS DOWN. ALL exit.)

SCENE 6

(Setting: The castle of the KRÁL. KRÁLOVNA & PRINCESS sit on thrones while several SERVANTS stand in attendance. LIGHTS UP. SERVANT #2 enters.)

SERVANT #2: Announcing: a messenger from the *Král!*

(PLAVACEK enters. He bows before the KRÁLOVNA and gives her the letter. She reads it out loud.)

KRÁLOVNA: "I have chosen this young man to be my son-in-law. Have him married to our daughter, the Princess, at once, before my return!"

(ALL gasp with astonishment, PLAVACEK is dumfounded. PRINCESS is examining him closely.)

KRÁLOVNA: This is most unusual! *(To Princess:)* Are you willing to marry him?
PRINCESS: Last night I dreamed about a young man who looks just like him...*Ano,* I will marry him!
KRÁLOVNA: Servants! Prepare for the wedding at once!

(LIGHTS DOWN. ALL exit except the KRÁLOVNA and SERVANT #3.)

SCENE 7

(Setting: The same, a few days later. KRÁL enters and is pacing, angry.)

KRÁLOVNA: But you commanded this marriage take place! Come, read your letter again!

(She gives him the letter and he reads it.)

KRÁL: *Ano,* it is my writing and my royal seal! Servant! Send my son-in-law to me immediately!

(SERVANT #3 exits and PLAVACEK enters.)

KRÁL: Plavacek, tell me, did you stop anywhere on your way to the castle?

PLAVACEK: *Ano.* I spent the night with three women who wore white dresses that shone like the moon.

KRÁL: Them again! Hmm...You must prove to me that you are worthy to be my son-in-law. Bring me *tri zlate vlasy Deda Vseveda,* three golden hairs of Grandfather Know All!

KRÁLOVNA: *(Shocked.)* Impossible!

PLAVACEK: *(Sadly.)* Ano. *Na shledanou!*

(PLAVACEK exits. LIGHTS DOWN. Change set: remove cottage and castle of the KRÁL; bring out ferry boat on one side of the stage.)

SCENE 8

(Setting: The shores of the Black Sea, a few weeks later. A ferryboat sits on one side, with a FERRYMAN inside. LIGHTS UP. PLAVACEK enters.)

PLAVACEK: *Dobry den,* good Ferryman!

FERRYMAN: *Dobry den!* Where are you going?

PLAVACEK: I'm going to get *tri zlate vlasy Deda Vseveda!*

FERRYMAN: You're going to Deda Vseveda! I've been waiting for a messenger such as you! For twenty years I've ferried people across the Black Sea and no one has helped me. If you'll promise to ask Deda Vseveda when I shall be released from my labors, I shall ferry you over!

PLAVACEK: *Ano,* I promise!

(PLAVACEK gets into the boat and they travel across the stage. On the other side, PLAVACEK gets out.)

PLAVACEK: *Na shledanou!*

FERRYMAN: *Na shledanou!*

(*PLAVACEK exits. LIGHTS down. Change set: Remove boat and set up backdrop set of cities and 2 thrones, one on either side of the stage.*)

SCENE 9

(*Setting: The cities and castles of SECOND & THIRD KRÁLS, a few weeks later. There is a city backdrop, center, on a free-standing wall – this could be the reverse side of another set. There is a throne on either side of the stage. LIGHTS UP. PLAVACEK enters from one side of the stage while BEGGAR enters from another side.*)

BEGGAR: Alms for the poor! Alms for the poor!
PLAVACEK: *Dobry den,* good Beggar!
BEGGAR: *Dobry den!* Where are you going?
PLAVACEK: I'm going to get *tri zlate vlasy Deda Vseveda!*
BEGGAR: You're going to Deda Vseveda! We've been waiting for a messenger such as you! Come, I will take you to our *Král!*

(*BEGGAR takes PLAVACEK to throne on one side of the stage as 2ND KRÁL enters and sits there. BEGGAR bows before the KRÁL.*)

BEGGAR: This young man is going to the castle of Deda Vseveda!
2ND KRÁL: Deda Vseveda! Hmm...We have here a tree which once bore the Apples of Youth. Whoever ate one of those golden apples became strong and healthy and lived forever! But for the last twenty years the tree has borne no fruit. If you'll promise to ask Deda Vseveda how to bring back the Apples of Youth, I'll reward you with riches!
PLAVACEK: *Ano,* I promise! *Na shledanou!*
2ND KRÁL: *Na shledanou!*

(*PLAVACEK leaves the castle of the 2ND KRÁL and continues on his journey through the performance space while 2ND KRÁL & BEGGAR exit. BLIND WOMAN enters and PLAVACEK comes up to her.*)

PLAVACEK: *Dobry den,* good woman!
BLIND WOMAN: *Dobry den!* Where are you going?
PLAVACEK: I'm going to get *tri zlate vlasy Deda Vseveda!*
BLIND WOMAN: You're going to Deda Vseveda! We've been waiting for a messenger such as you! Come, I will take you to our *Král!*

(BLIND WOMAN takes PLAVACEK to throne on the other side of the stage as 3RD KRÁL enters and sits there. BLIND WOMAN bows before the KRÁL.)

BLIND WOMAN: This young man is going to the castle of Deda Vseveda!

3RD KRÁL: Deda Vseveda! Hmm...We have here a spring out of which flows the Water of Life. If a person is dying and drinks of the magical spring, she becomes well at once! If a person dies and her body is sprinkled with the water, she becomes alive again!

But for the last twenty years the spring has stopped flowing. If you'll promise to ask Deda Vseveda how to bring back the Water of Life, I'll reward you with riches!

PLAVACEK: *Ano,* I promise! *Na shledanou!*

3RD KRÁL: *Na shledanou!*

(PLAVACEK exits. LIGHTS DOWN. 3RD KRÁL & BLIND WOMAN exit. Change set: Remove cities backdrop and thrones, replace with castle of DEDA VSEVEDA.)

SCENE 11

(Setting: The castle of DEDA VSEVEDA, a few weeks later. There is a bed or sleeping mat, a chair, and a place for PLAVACEK to hide, such as in a cupboard, or behind a wall. There may be an interior wall, decorated as a castle of sun and light. 3RD FATE enters and sits in chair, may be knitting. LIGHTS UP.)

NARRATOR: Plavacek traveled a long time, through many forests and cities. After a time he came to a beautiful green meadow, filled with flowers. In the center of the meadow stood a golden castle which was so brilliant with light that it seemed to be made of fire. It was the castle of Deda Vseveda!

(PLAVACEK enters. THIRD FATE looks up at him.)

3RD FATE: *Dobry den,* Plavacek! I thought you'd never get here!

PLAVACEK: *Dobry den!* I have come for *tri zlate vlasy Deda Vseveda!*

3RD FATE: Deda Vseveda is my own son, the shining sun himself! Every morning he flies out of here a little child and by midday he's grown into a man. When he returns in the evening he's an old grandfather! But I'm not your godmother for nothing – I'll see that you get *tri zlate vlasy Deda Vseveda!* You'd better hide in here *(Indicates hiding place.)* for when my son comes home, he may want to eat you for his supper!

PLAVACEK: Remember to ask Deda Vseveda for the answers to my questions!

3RD FATE: *Ano.*

(SOUND: howling wind or other noise.)

3RD FATE: He's coming! Hurry!

(PLAVACEK gets into hiding place as SOUND VOLUME comes UP. DEDA VSEVEDA enters as an old man, with gray hair and a beard. SOUND ENDS.)

DEDA VSEVEDA: I smell man's flesh! You have someone here, *Matka!*

3RD FATE: *Ne, ne,* my son.

DEDA VSEVEDA: Hmm...Well, I'm going to bed. *Dobrou noc!*

3RD FATE: *Dobrou noc!*

(DEDA VSEVEDA lies on bed or mat and goes to sleep. 3RD FATE leans over him, plucks out one of his hairs and throws it on the ground. SOUND: Guitar strum or other stringed instrument. DEDA VSEVEDA wakes up with a start.)

DEDA VSEVEDA: What do you want, *Matka?*

3RD FATE: I just had a strange dream about a tree with apples which make the old young again... But for twenty years the tree has borne no fruit. What must be done?

DEDA VSEVEDA: That's easy: A snake is hiding among the roots of the tree. Kill the snake and replant the tree in another place and it will bear fruit again!

(DEDA VSEVEDA goes back to sleep. 3RD FATE leans over him, plucks out one of his hairs and throws it on the ground. SOUND: guitar strum. DEDA VSEVEDA wakes up with a start.)

DEDA VSEVEDA: *(Irritated.)* What do you want, *Matka?*

3RD FATE: I just had a strange dream about a spring from which flows water that cures all diseases and brings the dead to life... But for twenty years the spring has run dry. What must be done?

DEDA VSEVEDA: That's easy: There's a frog stuck in the opening of the spring. Kill the frog and the water will flow again!

(DEDA VSEVEDA goes back to sleep. 3RD FATE leans over him, plucks out one of his hairs and throws it on the ground. SOUND: Guitar strum. DEDA VSEVEDA wakes up with a start.)

DEDA VSEVEDA: *(Angry.)* Why won't you let me sleep, *Matka?!!*

3RD FATE: I just had a strange dream about a Ferryman who rows people back and forth across the Black Sea ... But for twenty years no one has come to take his place. How long must he keep rowing?

DEDA VSEVEDA: That's easy: He's stupid! All he has to do is give the oars to the next passenger and jump ashore. Whoever gets the oars will be the next ferryman! Now let me sleep! I must rise early tomorrow and dry the tears of a princess. She weeps for her husband who's been sent by her father to get three of my golden hairs!

(DEDA VSEVEDA goes to sleep. 3RD FATE picks up the three hairs and smiles slyly. LIGHTS DOWN. LIGHTS UP. DEDA VSEVEDA wakes up, now a young man – he has taken off his gray wig and beard and now wears a brilliant, golden sun-ray headdress.)

DEDA VSEVEDA: *Na shledanou!*
3RD FATE: *Na shledanou!*

(SOUND: Wind howling or other noise. DEDA VSEVEDA flies out of the castle and exits. SOUND ENDS. 3RD FATE gets PLAVACEK out of hiding.)

3RD FATE: Here's *tri zlate vlasy Deda Vseveda!*
PLAVACEK: *Dekuji! Na shledenou!*
3RD FATE: *Na shledenou!*

(PLAVACEK exits. LIGHTS DOWN. Change set: Remove castle of DEDA VSEVEDA and replace with cities backdrop and thrones of 2ND & 3RD KRÁLS.)

SCENE 12

(Setting: The cities and castles of 2ND & 3RD KRÁLS, a few weeks later. 2ND KRÁL enters and sits on his throne while several PEOPLE enter and stand about. PLAVACEK enters.)

The Three Golden Hairs of Grandfather Know All 163

PLAVACEK: I've got your answer! Kill the snake at the root of the magic tree and replant it somewhere else!

(PEOPLE all exit in a hurry. A moment later they call out from backstage.)

PEOPLE: Hooray!!!

(PEOPLE enter, excited.)

PEOPLE: The Tree bears the Apples of Youth again!
2ND KRÁL: *(To Plavacek:) Dekuji!* I will reward you with twelve white horses loaded with as much gold and silver as they can carry!
PLAVACEK: *Dekuji! Na shledanou!*
ALL: *Na shledanou!*

(PLAVACEK exits. LIGHTS DOWN. 3RD KRÁL enters and sits on his throne while several PEOPLE enter and stand about. LIGHTS UP. PLAVACEK enters.)

PLAVACEK: I've got your answer! Kill the frog that blocks the magic spring!

(PEOPLE exit in a hurry. A moment later they call out from backstage.)

PEOPLE: Hooray!!!

(PEOPLE enter, excited.)

PEOPLE: The Water of Life flows again!
3RD KRÁL: *Dekuji!* I will reward you with twelve black horses loaded with as much gold and silver as they can carry!
PLAVACEK: *Dekuji! Na shledanou!*
ALL: *Na shledanou!*

(PLAVACEK exits. LIGHTS DOWN. ALL exit. Change set: Remove cities backdrop and 2 thrones. Replace with castle of the KRÁL and the FERRYMAN'S boat.)

SCENE 13

(Setting: The castle of the KRÁL, a few weeks later. The FERRYMAN sits in his boat which is placed on the other side of stage. KRÁL & KRÁLOVNA enter and sit on thrones, PRINCESS enters and stands

nearby and several SERVANTS enter and stand about. LIGHTS UP.
PLAVACEK enters. Everyone is shocked to see him.)

KRÁL: *(Angry.)* You again!!!
PRINCESS: *(Happy.)* Plavacek, you're back!

(PLAVACEK smiles at her, goes up to the KRÁL and hands him the
three hairs.)

PLAVACEK: Here's *tri zlate vlasy Deda Vseveda! (To Princess:)* And for
you, I have brought many fine horses with all the gold and silver
they can carry!
PRINCESS: But how did you get them?!!
PLAVACEK: They are rewards – I helped one *Král* regain the Apples of
Youth and I helped another *Král* restore the Water of Life!
KRÁL: *(Excited.)* Apples of Youth! Water of Life! I must have these trea-
sures for myself! I shall become young again and I shall live forever!!!

(During the following narration, KRÁL runs over to the FERRYMAN
who stands up in his boat.)

NARRATOR: The *Král* wasted no time. That very day he started off....

(FERRYMAN thrusts the oars at the KRÁL and runs away. KRÁL
paddles the boat to center stage and continues to row back and forth,
futilely, until the end of the play.)

NARRATOR:...and he hasn't returned yet, for he journeyed by way of
a ferry boat on the Black Sea. The Charcoal-Burner's son became
Král as the Fates had decided, and he and his *Královna* lived in
peace and happiness for many years.
KRÁL:*(Frustrated.)* Konec! At least, I hope it's the end!

APPENDIX A: VOCABULARY LIST
OF FOREIGN LANGUAGE

CZECH	ENGLISH	PRONUNCIATION
ano	yes	a'-no
Cesky Les	The Bohemian Forest	chess'-key les
Deda Vseveda	Grandfather Know All	day'-dah fcheh'-via-dah
dekuji	thank you	deh-koo'-ee
detátko	little baby	deh-tyet'-ko
dobrou noc	good night	doh'-bro nohtz'
dobry den	good day	doh'-bree den'
konec	the end	ko'-netz
král / královna	king / queen	krahl / krahl-o'-vnah
matka	mother	maht'-kah
na shledanou	good-bye, see you again	nah s-h-leh'-dah-no
ne	no	neh
tri zlate vlasy	3 golden hairs	tree zlah'-tay vlah'-see

SETS LIST

CHARCOAL-BURNER'S COTTAGE:
    bed
    chair
    sturdy table or other loft
    stepladder, chair, or other access to loft
    interior wall (optional)

KRAL'S CASTLE:
    2 thrones
    interior wall (optional)

FATES' COTTAGE:
    bed or sleeping mat
    3 chairs
    interior wall (optional – may use same as for Charcoal-Burner's cottage)

CITIES OF THE KRALS:
    free-standing wall of cities backdrop
    2 thrones (can use same as for Kral's castle)

DEDA VSEVEDA'S CASTLE:
    bed
    cupboard or other hiding place for Plavacek
    1 chair
    interior wall (optional – may be reverse of cities wall)

HOW TO MAKE THE SETS

FREESTANDING WALLS (for interior walls of Charcoal-Burner's cottage, Kral's castle, Fates' cottage, cities backdrop and Deda Vseveda's castle)
- very large, cardboard box
- cardboard cutting knife
- scissors
- heavy butcher paper
- tape or glue
- markers, crayons or paint with brushes
- colored paper or fabric (optional)

Cut box to create a freestanding wall with accordion folds. Cut butcher paper to size of the wall. *Tape or glue paper wall, including both sides if the set will be reversed (if cardboard is plain white, you can eliminate this step). Draw picture of the set on the wall with markers, crayons, or paint. Colored paper or fabric can also be used to decorate the wall, using glue or tape.*

THRONES
- 2 chairs
- large fabric pieces
- sturdy tape
- junk jewelry
- safety pins

Drape the chairs with fabric. Tape securely on back and bottom of chairs. Pin jewelry along the top and sides of the chairs.

APPENDIX C: PROPS

PROPS LIST

Blanket – for all bed scenes
Baby Doll
Baby Blanket
3 White Candles (or electric candles) OR White Wands – for Fates
Money – for Kral to give to Servant
Basket – large enough for doll
Long Fishing Line w/Hook for Basket
Fishing Nets (optional)
Drinking Cup
Shoulder Bag – for Kral
2 Letters
Quill Pen
Ferry Boat
Oars
Knitting (optional – for 3rd Fate)
3 Golden Hairs – use pipe cleaners

HOW TO MAKE THE PROPS

FERRY BOAT
- very large, cardboard box
- strong tape
- paint
- paint brushes

OR:

- butcher paper
- scissors
- glue
- markers or crayons

Fold and tape open both the top and bottom of the box. Paint the outside of the box. In lieu of paint, cover the outside of the ship with butcher paper and decorate with markers or crayons. Actors propel the boat by walking inside it while holding up the sides with their hands.

OARS

- 2 long poles or dowels, such as from a broom or mop
- 2 pieces of thick cardboard
- cardboard cutting tool
- tape
- paint, as needed

Draw a large circle, slightly oblong, on the cardboard, approximately 30 cm long. Use thick cardboard so it will not get easily bent. Draw a small column attached to the bottom of the circle, a few cm wide and long (for attaching to the pole), and cut out. Place the cardboard round near the top of the pole and wrap tape around the column, securing it to the pole. Paint as needed.

APPENDIX D: COSTUMES

COSTUME LIST

CHARCOAL-BURNER, CHARCOAL-BURNER'S WIFE, FISHERMAN, FISHERWOMAN, BEGGAR, BLIND WOMAN, & SERVANTS: Poor clothes – pants & shirts or skirts; may add vests, aprons, hats, etc.

KRALS & KRALOVNAS: royal outfit – pants & shirts or long dresses; with crowns

FATES: long, flowing white dresses or blouses & long skirts, with white veils; may have fanciful headbands or headdresses

PEOPLE: pants & shirts or skirts; may add vests, aprons, hats, and so on

DEDA VSEVEDA: pants & shirt, possibly with cape, all in yellow or gold and covered with gold glitter; a gray wig and gray beard, easy to remove; and a golden sun-ray headdress

HOW TO MAKE THE COSTUMES

CROWNS
- shiny, gold paper or cardboard
- scissors
- glue
- fake jewels (try a craft supply store)

Draw the crown shape, flat, on the gold paper or cardboard. If using paper, measure and cut a piece of light cardboard to reinforce it and glue it on the back. Glue jewels to the crown and allow time to dry. Cut a strip of the gold paper or cardboard 5 cm wide and staple to the crown, measuring the whole to fit around the actor's head.

SUN-RAY HEADDRESS
- plastic headband
- gold and yellow pipe cleaners

Wrap pipe cleaners around headband so that they are secure and stick out, like rays. Make sure the ends of the pipe cleaners will not poke the actor's scalp.

APPENDIX E: SOUND & MUSIC

SOUND:
Door knocking: wood blocks
Baby's cry: live or on tape
Deda Vseveda's entrance (wind howling): percussion instruments or noisemakers
3 Golden Hairs thrown on floor: guitar strum, or strum of other stringed instrument, or chimes

MUSIC:
Fates' Theme: some lovely, flowing music, on tape, CD or played live
Scene change music: any music played during scene changes, on tape or played live

VASILISA PREKRASNAIA
"Vasilisa the Beautiful"
(Russia)

This is one of the most ambitious of the play productions in this volume. It requires a lot of time for both rehearsal and production preparation...but the results are worth it! *Vasilisa* is a story with so much psychological and psychic depth that entire volumes can and have been written about it. It is a grand Russian tale of the Journey of the Soul: learning to trust one's Inner Voice (the magic doll), confronting Death and the Grandmother of Time (Baba Yaga), becoming Enlightened (receiving the Skull's light), and integrating one's own *anima/animus* (Vasilisa weds the Czar).

You will recognize Vasilisa's kinship with "Cinderella." It's likely these tales have a common ancestor and there are many versions of this story found all over the world. In some versions of *Vasilisa,* her magical helper is not a doll but a cat! Baba Yaga appears in many Russian folktales as the archetypal Ruler of the Underworld, that dark, scary place of fear we must all spend time in—as Vasilisa does—before we can come into full knowledge of ourselves. Ask your cast what they think is the meaning of these lines from the play, "Morning is wiser than evening" and "If you know too much you are soon old." Why does Baba Yaga not want anyone near her who is blessed? Why must Vasilisa feed her Kookla and what (metaphorically) is she feeding her?

While it carries much deep meaning, this story is also extremely entertaining for both the audience and the actors. The elements of magic and the special effects that are possible are fun to create and dramatically effective. A Russian song/dance can be included at the end. Creating Baba Yaga's skull fence can be a complex art project with magnificent results (or a simpler fence can be created which is also very effective).

Some Russian words are included in the script. Russian is written with the Cyrillic alphabet but in this script the Russian words are written with our own, latin alphabet. A related activity for this production is for the cast the learn the Cyrillic alphabet and spell their own names and simple words with it.

(By the way, the Stepsisters are not traditionally named Luidmilla and Svetlana—I made that part up.)

RUNNING TIME OF SHOW *(approximate):*
30-35 minutes
REHEARSAL TIME NEEDED:
18-20 hours
OTHER PRODUCTION TIME NEEDED:
8-12 hours
CAST SIZE:
Minimum: 9, plus Narrator (Except for those playing Vasilisa and Kook-la, all other actors can play more than one role.)

Maximum: 20-25 (There can be numerous Suitors and Servants, although these roles are very minimal. Some actors can play the horses of the Riders.)
GENDER OF CHARACTERS:
The gender of the main characters should be as in the traditional tale; however, Baba Yaga, Kookla, the Riders, and the Servants can be played as either female or male.

CHARACTERS:
NARRATOR
VASILISA – a young Russian girl
MOTHER – of Vasilisa
MERCHANT – Vasilisa's father
STEPMOTHER
LUIDMILLA – Vasilisa's stepsister
SVETLANA – Vasilisa's stepsister
KOOKLA – a magic doll
SUITORS – Vasilisa's admirers
WHITE RIDER – Bright Day
RED RIDER – Radiant Sun
BLACK RIDER – Dark Night
3 HORSES – of the Riders (optional)
BABA YAGA – a dark witch
3 PAIRS OF HANDS – servants of Baba Yaga
SKULL'S VOICE
OLD WOMAN – friend of Vasilisa
CZAR – Russian emperor
SERVANTS – of the Czar

SCENE 1

(Setting: Russia, a long time ago. The stage is set as the MER-CHANT'S house: center stage is a bed, easily removed. To one side are three chairs and a small table, behind which is a freestanding wall of the house interior. The reverse side of this wall is a dark forest scene which will be shown later. Somewhere on stage is a place for KOOKLA to hide, such as under the bed or behind one of the walls. The front door of the house can be pantomimed, or a real door or door set can be used. On the other side of the stage is BABA YAGA'S hut which for the time being is hidden by another freestanding wall of the house interior. The reverse side of this wall is also a dark forest scene which will be shown later. LIGHTS UP.)

NARRATOR: In a certain Czardom in Russia there once lived a mer-chant and his wife.

(MERCHANT & MOTHER enter.)

NARRATOR They had an only daughter who was so lovely that she was called *Vasilisa Prekrasnaia*, Vasilisa the Beautiful.

(VASILISA enters, carrying a bouquet of flowers which she gives to her MOTHER.)

NARRATOR: When Vasilisa was eight years old, her mother called her to her bedside one day.

(MOTHER lays down in the bed while VASILISA & MERCHANT exit.)

MOTHER: *(Calling weakly.)* Vasilisa!

(VASILISA enters.)

VASILISA: *Da, Mama?*
MOTHER: Vasilisa, dear, I am dying. I leave you my blessing and this little doll, this *kookla*.

(KOOKLA comes out from under the bed or from nearby.)

MOTHER: Listen and remember my last words: Always keep this little *kookla* with you and never show it to anyone. If trouble comes your way, feed the *kookla* and ask it's advice, and it will tell you what to do.

(MOTHER dies.)

VASILISA: Mama!

(Vasilisa cries. LIGHTS DOWN. VASILISA & MOTHER exit. Move or remove bed. KOOKLA hides somewhere.)

SCENE 2

(Setting: The same, a year or two later. LIGHTS UP.)

NARRATOR: When his wife died the merchant grieved and was lonely, but after awhile he decided to marry again. He chose a widow who had two daughters a little older than Vasilisa. The merchant thought the widow would make a good mother for Vasilisa .... but he was wrong.

(STEPMOTHER & STEPSISTERS enter and sit in the chairs during the following dialogue.)

STEPMOTHER: Where is that ugly Vasilisa?!!
LUIDMILLA: I hope she's become tired and sickly from all the hard work we make her do!
SVETLANA: I hope she's burned dark by the sun and wind from working in the garden!
ALL: *(Screeching.)* VASILISA!!!

(VASILISA enters.)

VASILISA: *Da?*
STEPMOTHER: Clean the fireplace!
LUIDMILLA: Sweep the floor!
SVETLANA: And no food for you until you scrub every pot in the kitchen!
VASILISA: *(Sighs.)* Da.

(STEPMOTHER & STEPSISTERS exit. VASILISA gets KOOKLA out of her hiding place and gives her something to eat from her pocket.)

VASILISA: Here, little *Kookla*, eat your fill, my dear!
And I'll pour all my troubles in your ear, your ear!
My stepmother is trying to drive me into the grave! Help me, *pujhalsta!*

KOOKLA: Don't worry, Vasilisa *Prekrasnaia!* Rest in the shade of the garden while I do all your work for you.
VASILISA: *Spaseeba!*
KOOKLA: *Pujhalsta.*

(LIGHTS DOWN. VASILISA exits while KOOKLA goes back to her hiding place.)

SCENE 3

(Setting: The same, a few years later. LIGHTS UP.)

NARRATOR: With her *Kookla's* help, Vasilisa had a good and easy life, becoming more and more beautiful. As she grew up, every young man in the village admired her and tried to woo her.

(SUITORS enter, and knock on the door to the house. STEPMOTHER enters and answers the door. Meanwhile, STEPSISTERS enter and sit in the chairs, preening themselves.)

STEPMOTHER: *Da?*
SUITORS: *Pujhalsta,* we want to marry Vasilisa!
STEPMOTHER: *(Disgusted and angry.)* Vasilisa? PAH!! I will not allow her to marry until my own daughters are married!
SUITORS: But they're so ugly, no one will marry them!
STEPMOTHER: Get out of here!

(She slams the door and SUITORS exit.)

STEPMOTHER: *(Calling out.)* Vasilisa! No supper for you tonight!

(MERCHANT enters, with traveling bag.)

MERCHANT: What did you say to Vasilisa?
STEPMOTHER: *(Flustered.)* Uh...uh...I said, she looks *super* tonight!
MERCHANT: *Da,* she always does! I'm glad you love her so much! Take good care of her while I'm away on business – I'll be gone a long time. *Dosvedanya!*
STEPMOTHER & STEPSISTERS: *Dosvedanya!*

(MERCHANT exits. STEPMOTHER goes over to her daughters.)

STEPMOTHER: Luidmilla, Svetlana, listen! We are moving at once to a house near the forest!

LUIDMILLA: But the witch, Baba Yaga, lives in the forest!

SVETLANA: Baba Yaga eats people as if they were chickens!

STEPMOTHER: *(Smiling wickedly.)* And if our dear Vasilisa becomes lost in the forest near Baba Yaga's house....

(ALL giggle with delight. LIGHTS DOWN. Change set to STEP-MOTHER'S house near the forest.)

SCENE 4

(Setting: The STEPMOTHER'S house at the edge of the forest, a few days later. 3 chairs and a table are set as before, with a large candle and yarn props on the table. The house interior wall in front of BABA YAGA'S hut is turned around to show a dark forest scene. There is some place for KOOKLA to hide outside the house, such as behind the forest wall. STEPMOTHER, STEPSISTERS & VASILISA enter and light the candle. LIGHTS UP.)

NARRATOR: As soon as they had settled in the new house, the Step-mother began sending Vasilisa out into the forest.

(STEPMOTHER & STEPSISTERS sternly point toward the forest. VASILISA, resigned, leaves the house and gets KOOKLA out of her hiding place. Meanwhile, STEPMOTHER & STEPSISTERS sit in the chairs.)

NARRATOR: But she would always take her little *Kookla* with her...

(VASILISA & KOOKLA go out into the forest and then KOOKLA points the way back to the house.)

NARRATOR:...and *Kookla* would always show her the way home and did not let Vasilisa go near Baba Yaga's hut.

(They return to the house. VASILISA puts KOOKLA back in her hiding place then goes into the house.)

STEPMOTHER & STEPSISTERS: *(Disappointed.)* You're back!

NARRATOR: One evening, the Stepmother gave out work to the three girls.

(STEPMOTHER stands and gives out yarn props while VASILISA sits in the third chair.)

STEPMOTHER: Luidmilla, you are to make lace; Svetlana, you are to knit stockings; and Vasilisa, you are to spin. I'm going to bed, but I'll leave one candle lit where you're working.

(She pantomimes blowing out lamps around the house while LIGHTS come down until most or all of the only light on stage is from the candle. She goes over to STEPSISTERS while VASILISA is looking the other way.)

STEPMOTHER: *(Stage whisper.)* Remember, girls! When you go to trim the wick of the candle, snuff it out instead!
STEPSISTERS: Da! *(Giggle.)*

(STEPMOTHER exits.)

LUIDMILLA: *(Loud and phony.)* Oh! I shall trim the wick of the candle! *(Blows it out.)* Oh, dear! The candle went out! What shall we do now?
SVETLANA: One of us will have to go get a light from Baba Yaga!
LUIDMILLA: I'm not going! I have enough light shining from my needles!
SVETLANA: I'm not going either for I have enough light shining from my needles!
BOTH: Vasilisa must go get a light from Baba Yaga!!

(They push her out the door and pantomime slamming it and locking her out.)

STEPSISTERS: *(Laughing.)* Dosvedanya!

(VASILISA gets KOOKLA out of her hiding place and desperately gives her something to eat from her pocket.)

VASILISA: Here, little *Kookla,* eat your fill, my dear!
And I'll pour all my troubles in your ear, your ear!
They're sending me to Baba Yaga's house for a light – Baba Yaga will eat me up! Help me, *pujhalsta!*
KOOKLA: Don't be afraid, Vasilisa *Prekrasnaia!* Keep me with you and Baba Yaga won't harm you.

(They exit together. LIGHTS DOWN, if any. Change set: The house interior wall behind the table and chairs is turned around to show a dark forest scene and is placed in front of the table and chairs.)

SCENE 5

(Setting: The forest, a few hours later. VASILISA & KOOKLA enter.)

NARRATOR: Vasilisa and *Kookla* entered the dark forest and walked all through the night. Then suddenly, a white horse and rider, dressed all in white, rode past them and it became light.

(WHITE RIDER enters, gallops across the stage, and exits. SOME LIGHTS UP. VASILISA & KOOKLA continue walking through the forest.)

NARRATOR: As they walked on a red horse and rider, dressed all in red, rode past them and the sun rose.

(RED RIDER enters, gallops across the stage and exits. MORE LIGHTS UP. VASILISA & KOOKLA continue walking.)

NARRATOR: All that day Vasilisa and her little *Kookla* walked through the forest and by evening they arrived at a clearing where stood Baba Yaga's strange little hut!

(Forest wall is moved to reveal BABA YAGA'S hut: There are 2-3 strong tables on top of which is an interior wall with 1 or more hatches cut into it, an oven, food and drink props, several large sacks, and a single skull that can be lit from inside. There may also be a long stick on which to carry the skull. A dark cloth hangs from the tabletops to the floor, downstage, on which are taped some large hen's legs. There is a small stepladder or other access to the tabletops. In front of the hut is a fence made of human bones and topped with human skulls. Inside the skulls are colored lights. The two sides of the fence meet in the center and can be opened and closed. There is a set of sharp teeth as the lock on the gate. 1 or 2 actors hide behind the fence in order to operate the gate. VASILISA & KOOKLA stand nearby and gape at the awesome sight.)

NARRATOR: Baba Yaga's hut twirled around and around on hen's legs! Surrounding the hut was a fence made of human bones, topped by human skulls. On the fence was a gate which had a lock made of a set of sharp teeth. Suddenly, a black horse and rider, all dressed in black, galloped up to the hut and disappeared and it became night.

(BLACK RIDER enters, galloping, and exits behind the hut. SOME LIGHTS DOWN. SKULL FENCE LIGHTS ON.)

NARRATOR: Then came a most fearsome noise, and all the trees began to groan and shake their leaves!

(SOUND EFFECTS; SETS SHAKE. VASILISA & KOOKLA hide somewhere.)

NARRATOR: Out of the forest came Baba Yaga, riding in a wooden mortar, swinging the pestle like a whip and sweeping away her tracks with a broom!

(BABA YAGA enters, as described above. The actor holds up the mortar with one hand and holds broom and sweeps with the other hand. The pestle is affixed to the mortar. When she arrives at the hut, SOUND EFFECTS & SETS SHAKING ENDS. BABA YAGA gets out of her mortar, puts down her broom, looks around, and sniffs.)

BABA YAGA: I smell Russian flesh! Who is here?!!

(VASILISA comes out of hiding and bows before her.)

VASILISA: It is I, *babushka!* My stepsisters sent me to ask you for a light!

BABA YAGA: *Harashow!* Stay and work for me awhile and then we'll see what is to be seen!

VASILISA: *Da.*

(BABA YAGA goes up to the gate.)

BABA YAGA: *(Commanding.)* My strong bolts unlock! My gates open wide!

(Gate opens by itself – operated by actors behind the fence. BABA YAGA goes into the hut. VASILISA surreptitiously gets KOOKLA out of hiding and brings her through the fence and hides her under the hut, then follows into the hut. Gate closes.)

BABA YAGA: I'm hungry! Bring me whatever's in the oven!

(Vasilisa goes to oven and brings back a huge tray of food and a big mug and BABA YAGA eats and drinks rapidly and noisily during the following narration.)

NARRATOR: There was enough food and drink for ten people and Baba Yaga ate and drank it all, leaving only a little bit of soup and a tiny crust of bread for Vasilisa.

(BABA YAGA finishes eating and pushes her tray away.)

BABA YAGA: Tomorrow, while I'm away, you must clean the yard, sweep the house, do the washing, and cook my dinner. Then take a sack of millet and clean out all the tiny black bits. If you don't do as I say, I will eat you up!

(BABA YAGA lies down and begins to snore loudly. VASILISA sneaks out of the hut and gets KOOKLA out from underneath. She gives her something to eat from her pocket.)

VASILISA: Here, little *Kookla,* eat your fill, my dear!
And I'll pour all my troubles in your ear, your ear!
Baba Yaga has given me impossible, hard work to do and if I don't get it all done, she will eat me up! Help me, *pujhalsta!*

KOOKLA: Never fear, Vasilisa *Prekrasnaia!* Say your prayers and go to bed, for morning is wiser than evening.

(VASILISA puts KOOKLA back under hut then goes inside and lies down. ALL LIGHTS DOWN; SKULL LIGHTS REMAIN ON.)

SCENE 6

(Setting: The same, the next morning.)

NARRATOR: After many hours the White Rider swept past and it became light.

(WHITE RIDER enters, gallops across stage and exits. SOME LIGHTS UP.)

NARRATOR: Then the Red Rider dashed by and the sun came up.

(RED RIDER enters, gallops across stage and exits. MORE LIGHTS UP. SKULL LIGHTS OFF. BABA YAGA goes out of the hut and stands before the fence gate.)

BABA YAGA: My strong bolts unlock! My gates open wide!

(Gate opens. BABA YAGA goes through it, picks up broom and gets

into her mortar. SOUND EFFECTS; SETS SHAKE. BABA YAGA exits. SOUND EFFECTS & SETS SHAKING STOPS. VASILISA gets up and looks around the hut. She then goes out of the hut and gets KOOKLA out from underneath.)

VASILISA: Dear *Kookla!* You have done all my work for me! *Spaseeba!*
KOOKLA: *Pujhalsta!* All you have to do now is set out Baba Yaga's dinner.

(VASILISA puts KOOKLA back under the hut then goes into the hut.)

NARRATOR: Toward evening Vasilisa put the food on the table and waited. Then the Black Rider passed by and it became night.

(BLACK RIDER enters, gallops across the stage and exits behind the hut. SOME LIGHTS DOWN; SKULL LIGHTS ON. SOUND EFFECTS; SETS SHAKE. BABA YAGA enters in mortar as before. When she arrives at the hut, SOUND EFFECTS, SETS SHAKING STOPS. She gets out of the mortar and puts down the broom. She stands before the gate.)

BABA YAGA: My strong bolts unlock! My gates open wide!

(Gate opens and she enters. Gate closes behind her. She goes into the hut and looks around.)

BABA YAGA: *(To Vasilisa:)* Is everything done?
VASILISA: See for yourself, *babushka!*
BABA YAGA: *(Looks around, is vexed.)* Da.

(BABA YAGA picks up some of the sacks on the floor.)

BABA YAGA: *(Commanding.)* My faithful servants!

(3 PAIRS OF HANDS appear through the hatches in the interior wall. VASILISA is amazed.)

BABA YAGA: Grind my millet!

(BABA YAGA gives the sacks to the HANDS and they disappear behind the wall. ALL LIGHTS DOWN; SKULL LIGHTS REMAIN ON. VASILISA & BABA YAGA exit backstage.)

SCENE 7

NARRATOR: The next day the same events occurred. Baba Yaga left the hut after giving Vasilisa an impossible set of jobs to do and again, her *Kookla* did all her work for her. This time, she was to take a sack of poppy seeds and clean the dirt off each one separately. When Baba Yaga returned that night and saw that this had been done, she again called for her faithful servants.

(LIGHTS UP. VASILISA & BABA YAGA enter and BABA YAGA picks up the rest of the sacks on the floor.)

BABA YAGA: My faithful servants!

(3 PAIRS OF HANDS appear through the hatches.)

BABA YAGA: Press my poppy seeds into oil!

(BABA YAGA gives the sacks to the HANDS and they disappear again. BABA YAGA sits down and VASILISA brings her food and drink. BABA YAGA eats and drinks while VASILISA sits nearby, silent.)

BABA YAGA: Why don't you speak to me?
VASILISA: I don't dare. But if I may, I'd like to ask something.
BABA YAGA: Go ahead, but remember: If you know too much, you are soon old!
VASILISA: Who is the White Rider?
BABA YAGA: Bright Day.
VASILISA: Who is the Red Rider?
BABA YAGA: Radiant Sun.
VASILISA: Who is the Black Rider?
BABA YAGA: Dark Night. All three are my faithful servants.

(VASILISA looks at the hatches in the wall where the HANDS appeared but says nothing.)

BABA YAGA: No more questions?
VASILISA: *Nyet, babushka.* You said yourself that if you know too much you are soon old!
BABA YAGA: *Harashow!* I eat those who are too curious! Now you tell me something: how do you manage to finish all the work I give you?
VASILISA: I am helped by my mother's blessing.
BABA YAGA: *(Jumping up, alarmed.)* Her blessing! I want no one near me who is blessed!

(BABA YAGA pushes VASILISA out of the hut. She picks up a skull that has a light in it and hands it to her. Skull may be carried on a long stick or handheld.)

BABA YAGA: Here's a light for your stepsisters! Now, get out of here!

(Gate opens. VASILISA manages to pull KOOKLA out of her hiding place and together they go out the gate and exit. ALL LIGHTS DOWN. Change set: Put the forest wall back in front of the hut. Move forest wall in front of the STEPMOTHER'S house: Turn it around to show house interior and place it behind the chairs and table as before.)

SCENE 8

(Setting: Stepmother's house near the forest, a day. STEPMOTHER & STEPSISTERS enter and sit slumped in the chairs, miserable. SOME LIGHTS ON. VASILISA & KOOKLA enter another area of the stage and stop.)

NARRATOR: By evening of the following day, they arrived back at the Stepmother's house. Thinking they could not still be without a light, Vasilisa was about to throw away the skull.

SKULL'S VOICE: DON'T THROW ME AWAY!!! TAKE ME TO YOUR STEPMOTHER!!!

(VASILISA puts KOOKLA in a hiding place outside the house and then enters the house. STEPMOTHER & STEPSISTERS act glad to see her.)

VASILISA: *Privyet.*
STEPMOTHER & STEPSISTERS: *Privyet,* Vasilisa!
LUIDMILLA: Since you've been gone we've had no fire!
SVETLANA: Whenever we borrowed a light from one of our neighbors, it went out as soon as we brought it home!
STEPMOTHER: But perhaps your fire may last!
NARRATOR: The eyes of the skull stared at the Stepmother and Stepsisters, boring into them and scorching them like fire!

(STEPMOTHER & STEPSISTERS are transfixed, in agony, by the eyes of the skull.)

NARRATOR: They tried to hide but the eyes followed them everywhere!

(SOUND EFFECTS: AS STEPMOTHER & STEPSISTERS try to run away from the eyes but are irresistably drawn to them and tortured by them. Slowly and dramatically they are killed by the eyes. SOUND EFFECTS STOP. LIGHTS ON.)

NARRATOR: The Stepmother and Stepsisters were burned to cinders by the stare of the skull! In the morning, Vasilisa buried the skull, locked the house, and taking her dear *Kookla* with her, she went into town.

(LIGHTS OUT. Change set: Leave 2 chairs and table and remove one chair. Remove the forest wall in front of BABA YAGA'S hut. Remove skull fence, oven, and food/drink props. Place 2 thrones on the table-top. Turn the interior wall of the hut around to show a castle wall and place down stage, in front of the thrones.)

SCENE 8

(Setting: OLD WOMAN'S house and CZAR'S palace. House interior is same as before; palace is 2 thrones on the tabletops, with a wall that for the time being is in front of the thrones, as an exterior wall with a window. OLD WOMAN enters house. LIGHTS UP.)

NARRATOR: Vasilisa went to live with an old woman who was a friend of her father's.

(VASILISA & KOOKLA enter, go up to the door and knock and OLD WOMAN comes to the door.)

OLD WOMAN: Vasilisa! *Privyet!*
VASILISA: *Privyet, babushka!*

(VASILISA & KOOKLA go into house with OLD WOMAN and all exit.)

NARRATOR: The old woman brought her some flax which Vasilisa spun into fine thread. Then her *Kookla* made her a special loom and Vasilisa wove all the thread into beautiful linen cloth that was so fine, it could be pulled through the eye of a needle, like thread. When it was finished, Vasilisa called the Old Woman to her.

(VASILISA, carrying cloth, & OLD WOMAN enter.)

VASILISA: *Pujhalsta, babushka,* sell this cloth and keep the money for yourself.

OLD WOMAN: *Nyet,* my child! Such fine linen is fit for none other than the *Czar!* I will take it to the palace as a gift!

(OLD WOMAN takes the cloth while Vasilisa sits in a chair. OLD WOMAN goes to the palace and stands below the exterior window, behind which is the CZAR.)

OLD WOMAN: *(Calling out.)* Your majesty!

CZAR: *(Through window.)* What do you want, *babushka?*

OLD WOMAN: I have something wonderful for you!

CZAR: *(Calling out.)* Servants! Bring the *babushka* to me!

(SERVANTS enter and escort OLD WOMAN into the palace. Meanwhile, the exterior wall is placed behind the thrones, so that it is now the interior wall and the thrones are visible. CZAR is seated in one of the thrones and his SERVANTS stand at attention. OLD WOMAN bows low before him, presenting him the cloth.)

OLD WOMAN: This is for you, your majesty!

(CZAR looks at the cloth carefully and is greatly impressed.)

CZAR: *Prekrasnaia!* What do you want for it?

OLD WOMAN: There is no price on such fine linen. I have brought it as a gift!

CZAR: *Spaseeba!* Servants! Have this cloth made into shirts for me!

SERVANT #1: But your majesty, there is no one who can do such fine work!

CZAR: *(To Old Woman:)* Babushka, If you can weave such linen, you should also be able to sew it into shirts!

OLD WOMAN: But it wasn't I who made the cloth, your majesty! It was a young woman named Vasilisa.

CZAR: Then have *her* sew me some shirts!

(He gives the cloth back to the OLD WOMAN and she goes back to her house.)

OLD WOMAN: *(To Vasilisa:)* The *Czar* wants you to make him some shirts!

VASILISA: I knew this would happen!

(She takes the shirts and VASILISA & OLD WOMAN exit.)

NARRATOR: Vasilisa locked herself in her room and sewed without stopping until she had made a dozen shirts. The Old Woman took them to the *Czar* while Vasilisa combed her hair and waited by the window to see what would happen next.

(OLD WOMAN, with a stack of shirts, and VASILISA enter. OLD WOMAN goes to the palace while Vasilisa sits in a chair. At the palace, the OLD WOMAN bows and hands the shirts to the CZAR.)

CZAR: *Harashow! Spaseeba!* Servants! Bring me the excellent seamstress, Vasilisa!

(SERVANTS go to house.)

SERVANT #2: *(to Vasilisa)* His majesty the *Czar* would like to meet the excellent seamstress who sewed him such fine shirts!
SERVANT #3: He wishes to reward you!
VASILISA: I knew this would happen!

(VASILISA & SERVANTS go to the palace. During the following narration the CZAR stands up when she arrives and, taking her by the hand, helps her sit on the other throne.)

NARRATOR: Vasilisa *Prekrasnaia* went before the *Czar.* Of course, he fell in love with her and ordered bells to be rung for their wedding.

(SOUND: BELLS. CZAR may place a crown on her head.)

NARRATOR: Vasilisa's father returned in time for the wedding...

(MERCHANT enters palace.)

NARRATOR: ...and, of course, her little *Kookla* was there for all the wedding dances and stayed with Vasilisa for the rest of her life.

(KOOKLA enters palace. MUSIC BEGINS: "Kalinka" or other Russian folksong. ALL dance/sing. MUSIC ENDS.)

ALL: *Conyetz!* The end!

(LIGHTS DOWN.)

APPENDIX A: VOCABULARY LIST
OF FOREIGN LANGUAGE

RUSSIAN *(spelled phonetically, with Latin alphabet)*	ENGLISH	PRONUNCIATION
Baba Yaga	old woman, a dark witch of Russian folklore	bah'-buh yuh-gah'
babushka	grandma, granny	bah'-boosh-kah
conyetz	the end	cone-yetz'
czar	king, emperor	tzahr
da	yes	dah
dosvedanya	good-bye, until later	doe s'vee-don'-yah
harashow	good	hah'-rah-show
kookla	doll	koo'-klah
nyet	no	n'yet
pujhalsta	please	puh-jhall'-uh-stuh
prekrasnaia	beautiful	pree-krah'-snay-ah
spaseeba	thank you	spah-see'-buh
"Kalinka" (song): Kalinka moia	my little snowball bush	kah-link'-ah moi-ah'
v'sadu yagoda malinka, malinka moia	my little one grows in the garden	v'saw'-doo yah'-go-dah mah-link'-ah, mah-link'-ah moi-ah'
Ay, liuli, liuli	"tra-la-la" *(idiomatic)*	aye' lee-oo'-lee, lee-oo'-lee

SETS LIST

MERCHANT'S HOUSE
> bed
> 3 chairs
> table (optional)
> 2 freestanding interior walls (reverse sides show forest)
> door set (optional)

STEPMOTHER'S HOUSE (use same as for Merchant's house)
> 3 chairs
> table
> freestanding interior wall (can be reversed to show forest and obscure view of house)
> freestanding forest wall (obscuring view of Baba Yaga's hut)
> door set (optional)

BABA YAGA'S HUT
> 2-3 sturdy tables
> dark cloth hung from tabletop to floor, facing audience
> chicken legs (paper or cardboard) taped to cloth
> stepladder or other access to tabletop
> freestanding interior wall, with hatches
> oven
> skull fence

OLD WOMAN'S HOUSE (use same as for Merchant's house)
> 2 chairs
> table (optional)
> freestanding interior wall
> door set (optional)

PALACE (use some of the same as for Baba Yaga's hut)
> 2-3 sturdy tables
> stepladder or other access to tabletop
> freestanding interior/exterior wall (can be reverse of Baba Yaga's interior wall)
> 2 thrones (use nice chairs, or decorate as described below)

HOW TO MAKE THE SETS

FREESTANDING WALLS (for house/hut interiors, forest scenes, palace interior/exterior, and skull fence)
- very large, cardboard box
- cardboard cutting knife
- scissors
- heavy butcher paper
- tape or glue
- markers, crayons or paint
- paintbrushes
- colored paper or fabric (optional)

Cut box to create a freestanding wall with accordion folds. For Baba Yaga's hut/palace wall, cut hatches/windows. To cut hatches, draw a square on the cardboard, large enough for the actor's arms and hands. Cut sides and bottom of square and fold up top to create a hatch door. They can also be opened from the top or sides. Cut 2 pieces of butcher paper to size of the wall. Tape or glue paper to both sides of the wall, including any hatches (if cardboard is plain white, you can eliminate this step). Draw picture of the set on the wall with markers, crayons or paint. Colored paper or fabric can also be used to decorate the wall, using glue or tape.

OVEN
- medium-sized box
- paint
- long, cardboard tube
- cardboard cutting tool
- paintbrushes

Cut an oven door so that it opens from the bottom. If you cut it so that the door opens from the top or sides, you will have to invent some sort of latch for it to stay closed. Cut a round hole in the top for the tube to fit through snugly as the stovepipe. Paint to resemble an oven with stovetop. Paint the tube black and insert it into the hole so that it rises up from the oven. Secure it by taping it from the inside.

SKULL FENCE
- 1 freestanding wall (see above for how to make)
- cardboard cutting tool
- extension cords (as needed)
- white & black paint
- small pieces of white cardboard
- papier mâché skulls (optional):
    - 10-12 balloons
    - bowl
    - 1/2 liter salt
- 2 strings of colored lights
- strong tape
- paintbrushes
- scissors
- newspaper or other paper
- 5-1/2 kgs. flour
- water

- white & black paint
- paintbrushes
- lengths of wood or sturdy cardboard, as needed
- wire or strong tape, as needed
- For hand-held skull:
  - 2 small, battery-operated, clip-on bicyclist lights
  - OR
    - 1 small flashlight
    - strong tape or wire, as needed

Make a large freestanding wall and cut in half lengthwise, to create 2 pieces of fence which are short enough so as not to obscure view of interior of Baba Yaga's hut. The two sides of the fence are placed so that they meet center and open and close as a gate the actors can come through (do not run lights across the opening between the two sides of fence). Another option is to make one fence wall and use one end as the gate. If using papier mâché skulls, cut the top of the fence so that it has sturdy spikes every 30 cm. or so on which the skulls can be affixed.

Draw large bones as fence pickets and paint them white. Paint the background black. If you're not making papier mâché skulls, skulls can be painted along the top of the fence.

For painted skulls, cut openings in the eyes for the lights. Tape the strings of lights along the back of the fence, with lights poking out of skull eye sockets.

Draw and cut a set of large, sharp teeth out of the white cardboard to be the lock on the gate. Tape the teeth to the ends of the fence where they come together.

Making paper maché skulls is a lot of work and a big mess, but the stage effect is worth it. The method I've described below for securing the skulls to the fence is the best I've found but it is still rather precarious. Think it through first and perhaps you will come up with a better solution.

To make papier mâché skulls: Blow up balloons to human-skull size and tie off the ends. In a bowl mix together flour, salt, and water to make a mix the consistency of pancake batter.

Cut or rip newspaper or other paper into long strips. Dip each strip into the mix and wipe off any excess. Apply it to the balloons until they are completely covered. To make sturdy skulls that will endure rehearsals and performances, cover balloons completely with a thick coating of paper maché. Allow to dry for 2–4 days. When completely dry, use scissors to cut out eye and nose sockets. With black paint or markers, draw mouth/teeth.

Cut a slit in the bottom of each skull and push it onto a spike along the top of the fence so that it rests securely; tape it to the back of the fence. If the skulls are still not secure, tape a small length of wood or strong cardboard to the back of each skull and to the back of the fence.

Tape the strings of lights along the top of the fence so that the lights poke out of the skull eye sockets. Secure the lights inside the skulls with tape or wire.

One skull is kept separate to be the one Baba Yaga gives to Vasilisa. Two bicyclist lights are affixed to the eye sockets, or a small flashlight is inserted through the back of the skull and taped or wired securely. Skull can be carried on a long stick or handheld.

THRONES
- 2 chairs
- sturdy taps
- safety pins
- large fabric pieces
- junk jewelry

Drape the chairs with fabric. Tape securely on back and bottom of chairs. Pin jewelry along the top and sides of the chairs.

APPENDIX C: PROPS

PROPS LIST

Bouquet of Flowers (plastic or paper, optional)
Blanket/Pillow (for Mother's bed)
Small Food Prop (for Kookla)
Travel Bag (for Merchant)
2 Sets of Neeldes & Yarn (lace-making & knitting)
Drop Spindle & Yarn (or pantomime spindle)
Large Candle, Matches (or use electric candle)
Skull (see above)
Long Stick (for skull – optional)
Large Mortar
Pestle (optional)
Small Broom
Tray of Food Props (for Baba Yaga)
Large Drinking Mug
Several Large Sacks (stuffed with paper – for millet and poppy seeds)
Several Shirts (folded, in a stack – or use a gift box)

HOW TO MAKE THE PROPS

MORTAR & PESTLE
- large cardboard box (sized for actor to walk in while carrying with one hand)
- a length of sturdy cardboard (pestle)
- cardboard cutting tool
- sturdy tape
- black or gray paint
- paintbrushes

Fold open the top and bottom of the box and tape to secure. Draw and cut a large

*cardboard piece as the pestle and tape securely to the inside of the box so that the
pestle sticks up over the top. Paint the box and pestle.*

APPENDIX D: COSTUMES

COSTUME LIST

VASILISA, MOTHER, KOOKLA, STEPMOTHER, STEPSISTERS &
   OLD WOMAN: traditional Russian costumes, or long skirts with blouses; may have vests or short jackets. Vasilisa should have an apron with a
   pocket in it and may also have a crown.
MERCHANT & SUITORS: pants & shirt; may have vests, jackets or hats
RIDERS: pants & shirts or leotard & tights in their respective colors; may add
   capes, jackets, boots or hats in their colors
HORSES: pants & shirts or leotard & tights in their respective colors; add
   ears and tails
BABA YAGA: dark witch costume; may include cape or hat
3 PAIRS OF HANDS: may have on long gloves in white, red and black
   (optional)
TSAR: traditional Russian royalty costume, or pants & shirt with decorated
   vest or jacket or a long, fancy robe. He could also have a crown
SERVANTS: pants & shirt, dresses, or blouse & long skirt; may add apron or
   tunics

HOW TO MAKE THE COSTUMES

CROWNS
   • shiny, gold paper or cardboard
   • scissors
   • glue
   • fake jewels (try a craft supply store)
*Draw the crown shape, flat, on the gold paper or cardboard. If using paper, mea-
sure and cut a piece of light cardboard to reinforce it and glue it on the back. Glue
jewels to the crown and allow time to dry. Cut a strip of the gold paper or cardboard 5 cm wide and staple to the crown, measuring the whole to fit around the
actor's head.*

HORSE EARS
   • colored construction paper – white, red and black
   • pencil
   • scissors
   • stapler

- light cardboard, glue (optional)
- markers, crayons, paint with brushes, (optional)
- fake fur, glue (optional)

Draw and cut out shape of ears with pencil on paper. Cut long strips of the same color, approximately 4 cm wide and long enough to go around the actors' heads with a 2-3 centimeters of overlap. Staple ears to strips, and staple strips to fit snugly around the actors' heads. You may want to reinforce ears and strips with a cardboard backing. Decorate as needed with markers, crayons or paint.

HORSE TAILS
- long strips, approx. 1 meter long, of colored chiffon or other light fabric: white, red and black
- scissors
- long, elastic strip or safety pins

Measure out three strips of fabric. Braid together and tie in a knot at either end. Tail is either pinned to back of actor's pants or tied to an elastic strip that is measured and tied to fit around actor's waist. The best place to pin the tail to pants is through belt loops. If you pin it directly to pants or shirt, it can rip the fabric if someone steps on the tail.

APPENDIX E: SOUND & MUSIC

SOUND:
  Baba Yaga's entrance/exit: noisemakers and/or percussion instruments to make weird or scary sounds
  Skull's eyes killing the Stepmother and Stepsisters: noisemakers and/or percussion instruments to make weird or scary sounds
  Wedding bells: hand bells
MUSIC:
  Song: *"Kalinka"* (included) or other Russian folksong (optional)
  Russian music to play during scene changes, live or on tape or CD

KALINKA
("Little Snowball Bush")

Russian folk song

Ka - lin - ka, ka - lin - ka, ka - lin - ka moi - a! V'sa - du

ya - go-da ma - lin - ka, ma - lin - ka moi - a! Ka - a! Oh -

Un - der- the pine tree, un - der- the green tree,

there I'll lay me down to sleep. Ah! Ay, liu - li,

liu - li, ay, liu - li - liu - li, there I'll lay me

down to sleep! Ka —

D.C. al Fine

BIBLIOGRAPHY

Bergeret, Annie, Editor. *Tales From China.* New Jersey: Silver Burdett, 1981.

Bowman, James Cloyd. *Seven Silly Wise Men.* Chicago: Albert Whitman & Co.

Haviland, Virginia. *Favorite Fairy Tales Told in Czechoslovakia.* Boston: Little, Brown & Co., 1966.

Haviland, Virginia. *Favorite Fairy Tales Told in Russia.* Boston: Little, Brown & Co., 1961.

Hilbert, Vi. *Haboo—Native American Stories From Puget Sound.* Seattle: University of Washington Press, 1985.

Minard, Rosemary, Editor. *Womenfolk and Fairy Tales.* Boston: Houghton Mifflin Co., 1975.

Te Kanawa, Kiri. *Land of the Long White Cloud.* New York: Arcade Publishing, Inc., Little, Brown & Co., 1989.

PAMELA GERKE has been Director and Playwright for Kids
Action ... ... inded it
in 1988 ... hildren's
plays, ... several
other s. d move-
ment s ... er time
betwee. ... Vomen's
Ensem e piano
instruc horuses
and for